# Real Food
### for
# Vegetarians

Carol Palmer

## foulsham
LONDON • NEW YORK • TORONTO • SYDNEY

# foulsham

The Publishing House, Bennetts Close,
Cippenham, Berks, SL1 5AP, England

*To my dear Mum and Dad, who have nurtured my love
of food and cooking and always supported me.*

ISBN 0-572-02501-7

Copyright © 2000 W. Foulsham & Co. Ltd.

Cover photograph © The Image Bank

Printed in Great Britain by The Bath Press, Bath

# CONTENTS

Introduction 4

Storecupboard Surprises 5

Notes on the Recipes 8

Starters 9

Main Meals 24

Side Dishes 64

Salads 82

Desserts 96

Quick Bakes 114

Index 125

# INTRODUCTION

Whether you are completely vegetarian or just enjoy the imaginative approach of modern vegetarian recipes, you'll find what you are looking for in this collection of straightforward, tasty and health-conscious recipes.

This book aims to show how a vast range of vegetarian dishes can be prepared from readily available ingredients. The recipes are a world away from the monotony of the restricted choice of the past: they are colourful and nutritious and bursting with flavour. Moreover, they take into consideration that the vegetarian cook has a life outside the kitchen and hence most of them do not take too long to prepare.

Many incorporate convenience and storecupboard commodities. However, this is never to the detriment of the final nutritional value, flavour and appearance of the dish, as these ingredients are creatively combined with a host of fresh ingredients.

*Real Food for Vegetarians* is a realistic approach to vegetarian cooking for the enthusiastic cook and food-lover. It is not a cordon bleu recipe book using delicatessen specialities, but when you see and taste some of the end results, you might be tempted to think it was!

# STORECUPBOARD SURPRISES

The secret behind conjuring up speedy yet impressive dishes is to have a well stocked storecupboard. Once upon a time this would have meant flour, sugar and a few other dried commodities, but today, with the vast range of convenience and preserved foods readily available, it is possible to have a comprehensive stock of standby foods. This means that tasty, nutritious, attractive and relatively inexpensive vegetarian dishes can be created at short notice.

Most of the recipes in this book include some basic storecupboard ingredients and some are almost completely constructed from what could be considered 'stock' ingredients. If a good storecupboard is always maintained, a substantial meal is always available. However, for a good vegetarian diet, storecupboard commodities are best used in combination with fresh ingredients.

The following is what I would consider a comprehensive list of storecupboard ingredients, from which many of the recipes in this book can be prepared. You may wish to add or take away from this list, depending on your personal taste and the likes and dislikes of those you regularly cook for.

## ESSENTIALLY DRY

◇ Plain (all-purpose) flour
◇ Cornflour (cornstarch)
◇ Baking powder
◇ Sugar – caster (superfine) and soft brown
◇ Cocoa (unsweetened chocolate) powder
◇ Semolina (cream of wheat)
◇ Custard powder
◇ Dried milk powder (non-fat dry milk)
◇ Dried breadcrumbs
◇ Dried beans and pulses – a selection of your favourites
◇ Pasta – any shape
◇ Rice

◇ Mixed dried fruit (fruit cake mix)
◇ No-soak prunes
◇ Walnut pieces
◇ Packet sauce mixes – white sauce and cheese sauce
◇ Cornflakes
◇ Pancake batter mix
◇ Pizza mix
◇ Stuffing mix – a garlic and herb combination is the most versatile

## ESSENTIAL FLAVOURS

◇ Black peppercorns, for grinding
◇ Salt – table and coarse, if possible
◇ Mustard powder – or made English mustard and a wholegrain mustard, if possible
◇ Vegetable stock cubes
◇ Tomato purée (paste)
◇ Soy sauce
◇ Honey – clear, not set
◇ Golden (light corn) syrup
◇ Jam (conserve) or jelly (clear conserve) – particularly redcurrant
◇ Garlic purée (paste)
◇ Vinegar – cider or wine vinegar and balsamic, if possible
◇ Extra virgin olive oil
◇ Selection of dried herbs – mixed herbs, thyme, oregano, rosemary and basil
◇ Selection of dried spices – curry powder, chilli powder, ground cinnamon, grated nutmeg, mixed (apple-pie) spice and ground ginger
◇ Chutney – a fruity variety such as apple, peach or red tomato
◇ Plain (semi-sweet) chocolate
◇ Lemon juice

# FRESH, CHILLED OR FROZEN

◇ Eggs, large
◇ Milk – whole or semi-skimmed
◇ Margarine – avoid low-fat spreads, which may not be suitable for cooking
◇ Butter
◇ Bread
◇ Hard cheese – a full-flavoured Cheddar is a good standby
◇ Cream cheese – plain and garlic and herb, if possible
◇ Grated Parmesan cheese – freeze and use as required
◇ Mayonnaise
◇ UHT double (heavy) or whipping cream
◇ Plain yoghurt
◇ Frozen puff pastry (paste)
◇ Frozen filo pastry
◇ Frozen sweetcorn (corn)
◇ Frozen peas
◇ Frozen chopped parsley
◇ Potatoes
◇ Onions
◇ Carrots

# CANNED AND BOTTLED

◇ Oil – vegetable, sunflower or corn
◇ Canned tomatoes
◇ Sun-dried tomatoes
◇ Baked beans
◇ Canned pulses and beans – keep a selection of your favourites
◇ Stoned (pitted) olives
◇ Canned fruit, particularly peaches, pineapple and any other favourites
◇ Carton/bottle of orange juice
◇ Condensed soups, particularly tomato and mushroom

# NOTES ON THE RECIPES

◇ Many of the recipes use dairy products. Vegans should either omit them or use vegan alternatives such as soya milk products. Make sure that cheeses, margarine and yoghurt used are suitable for vegetarians; they are usually clearly marked on the labels.

◇ Some recipes use processed foods such as canned soup, biscuits (cookies), baked beans, frozen pastry (paste) and stuffing mix. You should check the product labels to be certain of their suitability for vegetarians.

◇ Most gelatines are not suitable for vegetarians but a powdered form called Vege Gel is available. Again, check product labels carefully. Some alcoholic drinks use animal-derived products in their production.

◇ Wash and peel, where necessary, all fruit and vegetables before use. Ensure that all produce is as fresh as possible and in good condition.

◇ Some fresh ingredients may be replaced by storecupboard ingredients: for example, crushed garlic cloves may be replaced by garlic purée (paste).

◇ Where recipes call for herbs, ensure that they are fresh, if possible. If it is necessary to use dried herbs, use half the quantity stated.

◇ Can and packet sizes are approximate and will depend on the particular brand. Always use those nearest the size stated.

◇ Follow metric, imperial or American measures, and never be tempted to interchange.

◇ All spoon measures are level:    1 tsp = 5 ml
                                                   1 tbsp = 15 ml

◇ Eggs are large.

◇ All cooking times given in this book are approximate and the description of how the cooked product should look and feel should also be followed, e.g. 'Cook until soft and transparent'. Ensure that food is cooked thoroughly.

# STARTERS

This section includes a wide variety of delicious starters to suit every occasion from a family meal to a special dinner party. The soups are particularly versatile – light enough to be eaten before a main course but substantial enough to make a complete lunch or supper, if served with lots of crusty bread.

# ASPARAGUS PÂTÉ
## —— SERVES 4 ——

| | METRIC | IMPERIAL | AMERICAN |
|---|---|---|---|
| Can of asparagus, drained | 400 g | 14 oz | 1 large |
| Cream cheese | 100 g | 4 oz | ½ cup |
| Lemon juice | 2.5 ml | ½ tsp | ½ tsp |
| Tabasco sauce | 2.5 ml | ½ tsp | ½ tsp |
| Salt and freshly ground black pepper | | | |
| Melba toast or savoury biscuits (cookies), to serve | | | |

① Place all the ingredients in a blender or food processor and work to a smooth consistency.

② Spoon into small individual serving dishes and chill for about 30 minutes until firm.

③ Serve with melba toast or savoury biscuits.

PREPARATION TIME: 5 MINUTES PLUS CHILLING

# MELON WITH STEM GINGER
## SERVES 4

| | METRIC | IMPERIAL | AMERICAN |
|---|---|---|---|
| Ogen or honeydew melon | 1 | 1 | 1 |
| Stem ginger, finely chopped | 25 g | 1 oz | 1 tbsp |
| Syrup from the stem ginger | 60 ml | 4 tbsp | 4 tbsp |
| Sunflower seeds, toasted | 30 ml | 2 tbsp | 2 tbsp |

① Discard the melon seeds, then, using a melon baller, form the flesh into neat balls (reserve any odd pieces of melon for a fruit salad).

② Stir in the stem ginger and syrup.

③ Serve in individual sundae glasses, topped with the sunflower seeds.

PREPARATION TIME: 10 MINUTES

# MINTED PEA SOUP IN A MOMENT

—— SERVES 4 ——

|  | METRIC | IMPERIAL | AMERICAN |
|---|---|---|---|
| Vegetable stock cube | 1 | 1 | 1 |
| Small onion, finely chopped | 1 | 1 | 1 |
| Minted frozen peas | 450 g | 1 lb | 1 lb |
| Mint jelly (clear conserve) | 30 ml | 2 tbsp | 2 tbsp |
| Salt and freshly ground black pepper |  |  |  |
| Crème fraîche | 60 ml | 4 tbsp | 4 tbsp |
| Chopped fresh mint | 15 ml | 1 tbsp | 1 tbsp |

① Bring about 900 ml/1½ pints/3¾ cups of water to the boil and add the stock cube and onion.

② Add the peas, bring back to the boil and cook for about 5 minutes.

③ Cool the mixture slightly, then liquidise or process until smooth. Sieve (strain) to remove any skins.

④ Stir in the mint jelly, season to taste and heat through.

⑤ Serve in individual bowls with a tablespoonful of crème fraîche and a sprinkling of fresh mint on the surface of each one.

PREPARATION TIME: 5 MINUTES

COOKING TIME: 10 MINUTES

# SPICY CHICK PEA DIP WITH CRUDITÉS

—— SERVES 4 ——

| | METRIC | IMPERIAL | AMERICAN |
|---|---|---|---|
| **For the dip:** | | | |
| Can of chick peas (garbanzos), drained | 400 g | 14 oz | 1 large |
| Garlic cloves, peeled | 2 | 2 | 2 |
| Shallot, finely chopped | 1 | 1 | 1 |
| Chilli powder | 2.5 ml | ½ tsp | ½ tsp |
| A pinch of ground cumin | | | |
| Mayonnaise | 30 ml | 2 tbsp | 2 tbsp |
| Soured (dairy sour) cream | 45 ml | 3 tbsp | 3 tbsp |
| Salt and freshly ground black pepper | | | |
| Paprika, for sprinkling | | | |
| **For the crudités:** | | | |
| Large carrots, cut into long fine strips | 2 | 2 | 2 |
| Celery sticks, cut into 5 cm/2 in lengths | 5 | 5 | 5 |
| Large red (bell) pepper, cut into long fine strips | 1 | 1 | 1 |
| Large bag of tacos | 1 | 1 | 1 |

① Place all the ingredients for the dip, apart from the paprika, in a processor or liquidiser and process until smooth.

② Serve the dip in a bowl, sprinkled with the paprika. Surround with the crudités and tacos.

PREPARATION TIME: 10 MINUTES

# PIMIENTO AND AUBERGINE ROLLS

—— SERVES 4 ——

|  | METRIC | IMPERIAL | AMERICAN |
|---|---|---|---|
| Medium aubergines (eggplants) | 2 | 2 | 2 |
| Extra virgin olive oil | 45 ml | 3 tbsp | 3 tbsp |
| Can of pimientos, drained | 400 g | 14 oz | I large |
| Garlic clove, crushed | I | I | I |
| Spring onions (scallions), finely chopped | 3 | 3 | 3 |
| Garlic and herb cream cheese | 100 g | 4 oz | ½ cup |
| Torn fresh basil | 30 ml | 2 tbsp | 2 tbsp |

① Preheat the oven to 180°C/350°F/gas mark 4.

② Cut the aubergines lengthways into slices about 5 mm/¼ in thick. Lay in a roasting tin (pan) and brush with some of the oil.

③ Bake for about 15 minutes until softened.

④ Cut the pimientos into strips that match the size of the aubergine slices. Lay on top of the aubergine slices.

⑤ Combine the garlic, onions and cheese, then gently spread between the aubergine slices.

⑥ Carefully roll up the aubergine slices and secure with cocktail sticks (toothpicks). Brush with the remaining olive oil.

⑦ Bake for about 15–20 minutes.

⑧ Serve the roll-ups scattered with the torn basil leaves.

PREPARATION TIME: 25 MINUTES
COOKING TIME: 15–20 MINUTES

# WATERCRESS AND COURGETTE SOUP WITH STILTON

—— SERVES 4 ——

|  | METRIC | IMPERIAL | AMERICAN |
|---|---|---|---|
| Butter or margarine | 15 ml | 1 tbsp | 1 tbsp |
| Bunches of watercress, roughly chopped | 2 | 2 | 2 |
| Onion, chopped | 1 | 1 | 1 |
| Garlic clove, chopped | 1 | 1 | 1 |
| Vegetable stock cube | 1 | 1 | 1 |
| Medium courgette (zucchini), very finely diced | 1 | 1 | 1 |
| Cornflour (cornstarch) | 15 ml | 1 tbsp | 1 tbsp |
| Milk | 75 ml | 5 tbsp | 5 tbsp |
| A pinch of grated nutmeg |  |  |  |
| Salt and freshly ground black pepper |  |  |  |
| Stilton cheese, crumbled | 100 g | 4 oz | 1 cup |

1. Heat the butter or margarine in a large saucepan and sauté the watercress, onion and garlic for several minutes until softened.

2. Add about 600 ml/1 pt/2½ cups of boiling water and the stock cube and stir. Bring to the boil, then simmer for about 5 minutes.

3. Allow to cool slightly, then liquidise or process until smooth.

4. Add the diced courgette and simmer the soup for about 4 minutes until the courgette is tender.

5. Blend the cornflour with the milk, then stir into the soup. Cook, stirring, until slightly thickened.

6. Add nutmeg and seasoning to taste. Stir in the Stilton and serve immediately.

PREPARATION TIME: 10 MINUTES
COOKING TIME: 20 MINUTES

# CURRIED FILO PURSES
## —— SERVES 4 ——

|  | METRIC | IMPERIAL | AMERICAN |
|---|---|---|---|
| Oil | 10 ml | 2 tsp | 2 tsp |
| Small onion, finely chopped | 1 | 1 | 1 |
| Garlic clove, crushed | 1 | 1 | 1 |
| Canned or cooked green lentils | 45 ml | 3 tbsp | 3 tbsp |
| Button mushrooms, finely chopped | 4 | 4 | 4 |
| Cooked peas | 45 ml | 3 tbsp | 3 tbsp |
| Medium curry paste | 15 ml | 1 tbsp | 1 tbsp |
| Sheets of filo pastry (paste) | 8 | 8 | 8 |
| Butter or margarine, melted | 50 g | 2 oz | ¼ cup |
| Butter Bean and Tomato Salad (see page 91), to serve |  |  |  |

① Preheat the oven to 190°C/375°F/gas mark 5.

② Heat the oil in a saucepan and fry (sauté) the onion and garlic until softened.

③ Stir in the lentils and mushrooms, then add the peas and curry paste. Allow the mixture to cool slightly.

④ Take a sheet of pastry and cut it into four squares. Brush the squares with melted butter or margarine, then place on top of each other. Place a spoonful of the mixture in the middle of the square and squeeze the corners up to form a purse.

⑤ Repeat the process with the remaining pastry and filling, then place the purses on a greased baking (cookie) tray. Brush all over with melted butter or margarine.

⑥ Cook for 12–15 minutes until golden brown and crisp.

⑦ Serve hot with a Butter Bean and Tomato Salad.

PREPARATION TIME: 20 MINUTES
COOKING TIME: 12–15 MINUTES

# AVOCADO WITH SUN-DRIED TOMATOES
## —— SERVES 4 ——

|  | METRIC | IMPERIAL | AMERICAN |
|---|---|---|---|
| Ripe avocados | 2 | 2 | 2 |
| Hard-boiled (hard-cooked) eggs | 3 | 3 | 3 |
| Sun-dried tomatoes, roughly chopped | 8 | 8 | 8 |
| Capers in brine, drained | 10 ml | 2 tsp | 2 tsp |
| Extra virgin olive oil | 30 ml | 2 tbsp | 2 tbsp |
| Lemon juice | 10 ml | 2 tsp | 2 tsp |
| Salt and freshly ground black pepper |  |  |  |
| Ciabatta bread, to serve |  |  |  |

① Halve the avocados and remove the stones (pits). Make criss-cross cuts in the avocado flesh, then force the skin up to remove the rough cubes. Place in a bowl and retain the shells.

② Peel the eggs and cut each into eight pieces. Add to the tomatoes and capers and gently mix.

③ Combine the remaining ingredients and stir into the avocado mixture. Season with salt and pepper.

④ Pile back into the avocado shells.

⑤ Serve with warm ciabatta bread.

PREPARATION TIME: 10 MINUTES

# TOMATO AND BASIL SOUP WITH OREGANO

—— SERVES 4 ——

|  | METRIC | IMPERIAL | AMERICAN |
|---|---|---|---|
| Butter or margarine | 10 ml | 2 tsp | 2 tsp |
| Onion, chopped | 1 | 1 | 1 |
| Garlic cloves, crushed | 2 | 2 | 2 |
| Can of tomatoes with juice | 410 g | 14½ oz | 1 large |
| Water | 300 ml | ½ pt | 1¼ cups |
| Vegetable stock cube | 1 | 1 | 1 |
| Mini pasta | 50 g | 2 oz | 2 oz |
| Dried basil | 5 ml | 1 tsp | 1 tsp |
| Garlic and herb cream cheese | 50 g | 2 oz | ¼ cup |
| Salt and freshly ground black pepper |  |  |  |
| Single (light) cream | 30 ml | 2 tbsp | 2 tbsp |
| Crusty bread, to serve |  |  |  |

① Heat the butter or margarine in a saucepan and fry (sauté) the onion and garlic until softened.

② Stir in the tomatoes, water and crumbled stock cube and stir until the stock cube is dissolved.

③ Liquidise, using a hand blender or liquidiser, then return to the pan.

④ Bring to the boil, then stir in the pasta and simmer for 6–8 minutes.

⑤ Add the basil, then mix in the cream cheese. Season to taste, then reduce the heat and stir in the cream.

⑥ Serve hot with crusty bread.

PREPARATION TIME: 5 MINUTES

COOKING TIME: 6–8 MINUTES

# GINGERED LEEK FILO TARTS

—— SERVES 4 ——

|  | METRIC | IMPERIAL | AMERICAN |
|---|---|---|---|
| Butter or margarine | 25 g | I oz | 2 tbsp |
| Medium leeks, finely chopped | 2 | 2 | 2 |
| Chopped fresh root ginger | 10 ml | 2 tsp | 2 tsp |
| Salt and freshly ground black pepper | | | |
| Large squares of filo pastry (paste) | 8 | 8 | 8 |
| Extra melted butter or margarine, for brushing | | | |
| Crème fraîche | 60 ml | 4 tbsp | 4 tbsp |
| Snipped fresh chives | | | |

① Preheat the oven to 190°C/375°F/gas mark 5.

② Heat the butter or margarine in a saucepan and add the leeks and ginger. Stir until starting to soften, then reduce the heat, cover and cook slowly for about 5 minutes until the leeks are very soft.

③ Cut each square of pastry into four smaller squares.

④ Grease a bun tin (patty pan) and put in a small square of pastry, pushing down gently. Brush with melted butter or margarine, place a second square on top, at a slight angle to the first. Continue this process with two more small squares and brush with melted butter or margarine. Line eight bun tins to form eight tart shells.

⑤ Divide the leek mixture between the eight tart shells.

⑥ Bake for about 10–12 minutes or until the filo pastry is crisp and brown.

⑦ Combine the crème fraîche with the chives.

⑧ Serve the tarts warm with spoonfuls of the crème fraîche mixture.

PREPARATION TIME: 15 MINUTES
COOKING TIME: 10–12 MINUTES

# CAULIFLOWER AND WALNUT SOUP

—— SERVES 4 ——

|  | METRIC | IMPERIAL | AMERICAN |
|---|---|---|---|
| Medium cauliflower | I | I | I |
| Butter or margarine | 50 g | 2 oz | ¼ cup |
| Small onion, finely chopped | I | I | I |
| Vegetable stock cube | I | I | I |
| Walnuts, chopped | 50 g | 2 oz | ½ cup |
| Cornflour (cornstarch) | 30 ml | 2 tbsp | 2 tbsp |
| Single (light) cream | 150 ml | ¼ pt | ⅔ cup |
| Salt and freshly ground black pepper | | | |
| A few chopped walnuts, to garnish | | | |

① Cut the cauliflower up into small pieces, chopping the stalk finely and discarding any very tough parts.

② Heat the butter or margarine in a large saucepan and add the cauliflower and onion.

③ Cook, stirring, until the onion has started to soften.

④ Add about 600 ml/1 pt/2½ cups of boiling water and the stock cube. Simmer for 30–40 minutes until the cauliflower is quite tender.

⑤ Add the walnuts and cook for a further 10 minutes.

⑥ Allow the mixture to cool slightly, then blend or process and return to the saucepan.

⑦ Blend the cornflour with a little of the cream and pour the remaining cream into the soup.

⑧ Heat gently and stir in the cornflour mixture a little at a time until the required thickness is reached. Adjust the seasoning to taste.

⑨ Serve hot garnished with a few chopped walnuts.

PREPARATION TIME: 10 MINUTES
COOKING TIME: 50 MINUTES

# CHEESY COURGETTES WITH REDCURRANT SAUCE

—— SERVES 4 ——

|  | METRIC | IMPERIAL | AMERICAN |
|---|---|---|---|
| Dried breadcrumbs | 100 g | 4 oz | 1 cup |
| Finely grated strong hard cheese | 30 ml | 2 tbsp | 2 tbsp |
| Freshly grated Parmesan cheese | 15 ml | 1 tbsp | 1 tbsp |
| Salt and freshly ground black pepper |  |  |  |
| Medium courgettes (zucchini), cut into 5 cm/2 in sticks | 2 | 2 | 2 |
| Egg, lightly beaten | 1 | 1 | 1 |
| Oil | 45 ml | 3 tbsp | 3 tbsp |
| Redcurrant jelly (clear conserve) | 45 ml | 3 tbsp | 3 tbsp |
| Port | 10 ml | 2 tsp | 2 tsp |

① Combine the breadcrumbs, cheeses and salt and pepper.

② Dip the courgette sticks into the egg, then into the breadcrumb mixture.

③ Heat the oil in a frying pan (skillet) and fry (sauté) the courgettes, turning once, until they are lightly browned and crisp. Keep warm.

④ Place the redcurrant jelly and port in a saucepan and heat, stirring, until combined.

⑤ Serve the courgette sticks warm with a small spoonful of sauce for dipping.

PREPARATION TIME: 5 MINUTES
COOKING TIME: 10 MINUTES

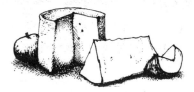

# MASCARPONE PEARS WITH BRANDY PISTACHIOS

—— SERVES 4 ——

|  | METRIC | IMPERIAL | AMERICAN |
|---|---|---|---|
| Mascarpone cheese | 225 g | 8 oz | I cup |
| Pistachio nuts, roughly chopped | 50 g | 2 oz | ½ cup |
| Green peppercorns, roughly crushed | 10 ml | 2 tsp | 2 tsp |
| Salt | | | |
| Canned pear halves, drained | 8 | 8 | 8 |
| Brandy | 30 ml | 2 tbsp | 2 tbsp |
| **For decoration:** | | | |
| Red salad leaves | 8 | 8 | 8 |
| Pistachio nuts, finely chopped | 10 ml | 2 tsp | 2 tsp |

① Combine the cheese with the nuts and peppercorns and add salt to taste.

② Divide the mixture between the pear halves and spoon into the cavities.

③ Drizzle the brandy all over the filled pear halves.

④ Arrange two pear halves for each serving on a few red salad leaves sprinkled with the chopped pistachio nuts.

PREPARATION TIME: 5 MINUTES

# CIDER SOUP WITH PAPRIKA
## —— SERVES 4 ——

|  | METRIC | IMPERIAL | AMERICAN |
|---|---|---|---|
| Onions, finely chopped | 2 | 2 | 2 |
| Butter or margarine | 50 g | 2 oz | ¼ cup |
| Plain (all-purpose) flour | 40 g | 1½ oz | ⅓ cup |
| Milk | 300 ml | ½ pt | 1¼ cups |
| Vegetable stock | 300 ml | ½ pt | 1¼ cups |
| Medium dry cider | 300 ml | ½ pt | 1¼ cups |
| Salt and freshly ground black pepper | | | |
| A pinch of grated nutmeg | | | |
| Cheddar cheese, grated | 225 g | 8 oz | 2 cups |
| Paprika | | | |
| Warm crusty bread, to serve | | | |

① Fry (sauté) the onions in the butter or margarine until tender.

② Add the flour and cook gently for 1 minute, stirring well.

③ Pour in the milk, stock and cider. Add the seasoning and nutmeg and bring to the boil, stirring.

④ Add the cheese and stir until melted.

⑤ Serve with a sprinkling of paprika and plenty of warm crusty bread.

PREPARATION TIME: 5 MINUTES
COOKING TIME: 10 MINUTES

# OLIVE AND AVOCADO VOL-AU-VENTS
## —— SERVES 4 ——

| | METRIC | IMPERIAL | AMERICAN |
|---|---|---|---|
| Ready-made vol-au-vent cases | 12 | 12 | 12 |
| Large ripe avocado, peeled, stoned (pitted) and roughly chopped | 1 | 1 | 1 |
| Small garlic clove, peeled | 1 | 1 | 1 |
| Can of stoned (pitted) olives in brine | 185 g | 6½ oz | 1 small |
| Extra virgin olive oil | 10 ml | 2 tsp | 2 tsp |
| Balsamic or raspberry vinegar | 10 ml | 2 tsp | 2 tsp |
| Salt and freshly ground black pepper | | | |

① Warm the vol-au-vent cases in a hot oven for a few minutes and keep warm.

② Place the avocado, garlic, all but six of the olives, 10 ml/2 tsp of the olive brine, the olive oil, vinegar, salt and pepper in a processor or liquidiser and blend until a fairly coarse consistency is reached.

③ Spoon the mixture into the warm vol-au-vent cases.

④ Halve the six reserved olives and use to decorate the vol-au-vents.

PREPARATION TIME: 5 MINUTES

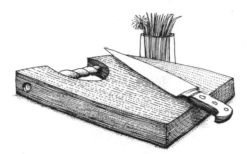

# MAIN MEALS

There's something for everyone in this section: children's favourites such as sausages, pancakes and rarebit; casseroles and turnovers for the heartier eaters; and even a few with more exotic ingredients for the adventurous amongst you. Do try to mix and match colours and, particularly, textures.

Warm, fresh bread and a crisp salad will provide an excellent accompaniment to almost any of these dishes, but serving suggestions are included with many of the recipes. However, these are just ideas and you will find lots more to choose from in the sections on side dishes and salads.

# PERSIAN SQUASH WITH PEPPERS
## —— SERVES 4 ——

| | METRIC | IMPERIAL | AMERICAN |
|---|---|---|---|
| Medium butternut squash, peeled, seeded and diced | I | I | I |
| Can of green lentils, drained, retaining the brine | 400 g | 14 oz | I large |
| Garlic cloves, crushed | 2 | 2 | 2 |
| Onion, chopped | I | I | I |
| Lemon juice | 30 ml | 2 tbsp | 2 tbsp |
| Tomato purée (paste) | 30 ml | 2 tbsp | 2 tbsp |
| Vegetable stock, made with one stock cube | 150 ml | ¼ pt | ⅔ cup |
| Ground cinnamon | 10 ml | 2 tsp | 2 tsp |
| Ground allspice | 5 ml | I tsp | I tsp |
| Salt and freshly ground black pepper | | | |
| Raisins | 25 g | I oz | 2 tbsp |
| Large red (bell) peppers, seeded and halved lengthwise | 4 | 4 | 4 |
| Boiled wild rice, to serve | | | |

① Preheat the oven to 200°C/400°F/gas mark 6.

② Place the squash with all the other ingredients except the peppers in a saucepan and simmer for about 15 minutes or until the squash is just tender, adding a little more water if the mixture dries out.

③ Place the pepper halves, cut side up, in an ovenproof dish and divide the squash mixture between them.

④ Cover with foil and cook for about 30 minutes or until the peppers are soft.

⑤ Serve hot with wild rice.

PREPARATION TIME: 15 MINUTES
COOKING TIME: 30 MINUTES

# WINTER CASSEROLE WITH MUSTARD DUMPLINGS

## —— SERVES 4 ——

| | METRIC | IMPERIAL | AMERICAN |
|---|---|---|---|
| **For the casserole:** | | | |
| Oil | 30 ml | 2 tbsp | 2 tbsp |
| Onions, quartered | 2 | 2 | 2 |
| Garlic cloves, halved | 3 | 3 | 3 |
| Carrots, cut into 4 chunks | 3 | 3 | 3 |
| Small swede (rutabaga), diced | ½ | ½ | ½ |
| Large parsnip, diced | I | I | I |
| Large celery sticks, chopped | 3 | 3 | 3 |
| Button mushrooms, quartered | 8 | 8 | 8 |
| Sweet cider | 300 ml | ½ pt | I ¼ cups |
| Vegetable stock, made with one vegetable stock cube | 300 ml | ½ pt | I ¼ cups |
| Can of chopped tomatoes | 410 g | 14½ oz | I large |
| No-soak vegetable casserole mix | 25 g | I oz | ¼ cup |
| Bay leaves | 2 | 2 | 2 |
| Dried mixed herbs | 5 ml | I tsp | I tsp |
| Salt and freshly ground black pepper | | | |
| **For the dumplings:** | | | |
| Self-raising (self-rising) flour | 100 g | 4 oz | I cup |
| A pinch of salt | | | |
| Vegetable suet | 50 g | 2 oz | ½ cup |
| Dijon mustard | 15 ml | I tbsp | I tbsp |
| A little water | | | |
| Chopped fresh parsley, to garnish | | | |
| Steamed broccoli, to serve | | | |

① Preheat the oven to 180°C/350°F/gas mark 4.

② Heat the oil in a large flameproof casserole (Dutch oven) and add the onions, garlic, carrots, swede, parsnip and celery. Stir well. Cover, reduce the heat slightly and leave to sweat for about 5 minutes.

③ Stir in the remaining casserole ingredients. Cover and place in the oven for about 45 minutes until the vegetables are tender.

④ While the casserole is cooking, make the dumplings. Sift the flour and salt into a bowl and mix in the suet. Blend the mustard with about 15 ml/1 tbsp of water, then stir gradually into the flour mixture to give a soft but not sticky dough. Gently form into eight small balls.

⑤ Place the dumplings on the top of the casserole and return to the oven for about 20 minutes or until the dumplings are risen and browned.

⑥ Garnish with parsley and serve hot with steamed broccoli.

PREPARATION TIME: 20 MINUTES
COOKING TIME: 1 HOUR 10 MINUTES

## BABY BEETROOTS IN A CHEESE SAUCE

—— SERVES 4 ——

|  | METRIC | IMPERIAL | AMERICAN |
| --- | --- | --- | --- |
| Baby beetroots (red beets), washed but not peeled or trimmed | 450 g | 1 lb | 1 lb |
| Packet of cheese sauce mix | 20 g | ¾ oz | 1 small |
| Milk, according to packet directions |  |  |  |
| Mozzarella cheese, cubed | 50 g | 2 oz | ½ cup |
| Parmesan cheese, finely grated | 25 g | 1 oz | ¼ cup |
| Creamed potatoes and a crisp salad, to serve |  |  |  |

① Place the beetroots in a pan and cover with water. Bring to the boil and cook for 25 minutes until tender. Drain.

② Preheat the oven to 180°C/350°F/gas mark 4.

③ Peel and trim the beetroots and place in an ovenproof dish.

④ Make the cheese sauce with the milk according to the packet instructions. Pour the sauce over the beetroots and sprinkle with Mozzarella and Parmesan.

⑤ Bake for about 25 minutes until golden and bubbling.

⑥ Serve with creamed potatoes and a crisp salad.

PREPARATION TIME: 35 MINUTES
COOKING TIME: 25 MINUTES

# MILD CURRIED RISOTTO WITH CUCUMBER RAITA

—— SERVES 4 ——

|  | METRIC | IMPERIAL | AMERICAN |
|---|---|---|---|
| Oil | 30 ml | 2 tbsp | 2 tbsp |
| Large onion, roughly chopped | I | I | I |
| Garlic cloves, crushed | 2 | 2 | 2 |
| Red (bell) pepper, seeded and diced | I | I | I |
| Long-grain rice | 350 g | 12 oz | I ½ cups |
| Can of tomatoes with juice | 410 g | 14½ oz | I large |
| Courgette (zucchini), diced | I | I | I |
| Button mushrooms, quartered | 100 g | 4 oz | 4 oz |
| Vegetable stock cube | I | I | I |
| Medium curry powder | 15 ml | I tbsp | I tbsp |
| Chilli powder | 2.5 ml | ½ tsp | ½ tsp |
| Ground cumin | 2.5 ml | ½ tsp | ½ tsp |
| Ground turmeric | 2.5 ml | ½ tsp | ½ tsp |
| Salt and freshly ground black pepper |  |  |  |
| **For the raita:** |  |  |  |
| Cucumber, peeled and grated | ½ | ½ | ½ |
| Chopped fresh mint | 30 ml | 2 tbsp | 2 tbsp |
| Plain yoghurt | 300 ml | ½ pt | I ¼ cups |
| Freshly ground black pepper |  |  |  |

① Heat the oil in a large frying pan (skillet) or wok and fry (sauté) the onion, garlic and red pepper until soft.

② Add the rice and stir for 4 minutes until transparent.

③ Stir in the tomatoes and juice with about 900 ml/1½ pts/ 3¾ cups of water. Bring to the boil, then stir in the remaining risotto ingredients.

④ Cover and simmer for 20–25 minutes until the rice is tender and most of the liquid has been absorbed.

⑤ Combine all the raita ingredients and season to taste.

⑥ Serve the risotto hot with raita on the side.

PREPARATION TIME: 15 MINUTES
COOKING TIME: 20–25 MINUTES

# SPICED BEAN AND AVOCADO RAFTS

—— SERVES 4 ——

|  | METRIC | IMPERIAL | AMERICAN |
|---|---|---|---|
| Extra virgin olive oil | 30 ml | 2 tbsp | 2 tbsp |
| Garlic cloves, crushed | 2 | 2 | 2 |
| Slices of ciabatta bread, 2 cm/¾ in thick | 8 | 8 | 8 |
| Can of mixed beans in chilli sauce | 400 g | 14 oz | 1 large |
| Small avocados, peeled, stoned (pitted) and sliced | 2 | 2 | 2 |
| Salt and freshly ground black pepper | | | |
| Feta cheese, diced | 100 g | 4 oz | ½ cup |
| Chopped fresh parsley (optional) | 30 ml | 2 tbsp | 2 tbsp |
| Green salad, to serve | | | |

① Preheat the grill (broiler) on the highest setting.

② Combine the olive oil and garlic and brush over one side of all the slices of bread.

③ Lightly toast the bread, oiled side up.

④ Brush the other sides with the oil mixture and lightly toast.

⑤ Warm the beans in a saucepan, then divide between the bread slices.

⑥ Arrange the avocado slices on top of the beans. Season the slices well, then top with the Feta cubes.

⑦ Place under the hot grill for a few minutes to heat the avocado and cheese through.

⑧ Serve hot sprinkled with the parsley, if liked, and accompanied by a simple green salad.

PREPARATION TIME: 10 MINUTES
COOKING TIME: 10 MINUTES

# CELERY AND SWEETCORN PANCAKES

## —— SERVES 4 ——

|  | METRIC | IMPERIAL | AMERICAN |
|---|---|---|---|
| Packet of batter mix | 130 g | 4 oz | 1 |
| Milk or water, according to packet instructions |  |  |  |
| A little oil |  |  |  |
| Butter or margarine | 15 ml | 1 tbsp | 1 tbsp |
| Onion, chopped | 1 | 1 | 1 |
| Large celery sticks, thinly sliced | 4 | 4 | 4 |
| Can of sweetcorn (corn) with (bell) peppers, drained | 400 g | 14 oz | 1 large |
| Can of carbonara sauce | 400 g | 14 oz | 1 large |
| Salt and freshly ground black pepper |  |  |  |
| Strong Cheddar cheese, grated | 100 g | 4 oz | 1 cup |
| Salted peanuts, lightly crushed | 50 g | 2 oz | ½ cup |
| Butter Bean and Tomato Salad (see page 91), to serve |  |  |  |

① Preheat the oven to 190°C/375°F/gas mark 5.

② Make the pancake batter according to the packet instructions.

③ Heat a small amount of oil in a frying pan (skillet) and cook the pancakes according to the packet instructions, adding more oil when necessary. (The packet mix should make about eight pancakes.)

④ Heat the butter or margarine in a saucepan and add the onion and celery. Cook until softened.

⑤ Stir in the sweetcorn and half the carbonara sauce and heat through. Season to taste.

⑥ Place a spoonful of the mixture on the centre of each pancake. Roll the pancakes up and place in an ovenproof dish with the ends tucked under to hold in the filling.

⑦ Pour the remaining sauce over the pancakes, then top with the grated cheese and crushed peanuts.

⑧ Place in the oven and bake for about 20 minutes or until the cheese is melted and browned and the pancakes heated through.

⑨ Serve with a Butter Bean and Tomato Salad.

PREPARATION TIME: 20 MINUTES
COOKING TIME: 20 MINUTES

# MIXED MUSHROOMS IN RED WINE SAUCE
—— SERVES 4 ——

|  | METRIC | IMPERIAL | AMERICAN |
|---|---|---|---|
| Butter or margarine | 50 g | 2 oz | ¼ cup |
| Garlic clove, crushed | I | I | I |
| Red onions, thinly sliced | 2 | 2 | 2 |
| Small button mushrooms | 225 g | 8 oz | 8 oz |
| Shiitake mushrooms | 175 g | 6 oz | 6 oz |
| Oyster mushrooms | 175 g | 6 oz | 6 oz |
| Large mushrooms, thickly sliced | 175 g | 6 oz | 6 oz |
| Can of red wine cook-in sauce | 400 g | 14 oz | I large |
| Whole black peppercorns, crushed | 5 ml | I tsp | I tsp |
| Salt | | | |
| Buttered tagliatelle, to serve | | | |
| Chopped fresh parsley, to garnish | | | |

① Heat the butter or margarine in a large saucepan and add the garlic and onion. Cook until the onion is soft.

② Add the mushrooms and cook until the juices start to run.

③ Gently stir in the remaining mushrooms and cook for a few minutes.

④ Add the red wine sauce and peppercorns. Stir well, then cover the pan and simmer for about 15–20 minutes or until the mushrooms are very soft. Add salt to taste.

⑤ Serve with buttered tagliatelle and a sprinkling of chopped fresh parsley.

PREPARATION TIME: 10 MINUTES
COOKING TIME: 15–20 MINUTES

# CARROT AND HERB SAUSAGES
## —— SERVES 4 ——

|  | METRIC | IMPERIAL | AMERICAN |
|---|---|---|---|
| Carrots, sliced | 450 g | 1 lb | 1 lb |
| A little oil | | | |
| Onion, finely chopped | 1 | 1 | 1 |
| Garlic clove, crushed | 1 | 1 | 1 |
| Fresh wholemeal breadcrumbs | 150 g | 5 oz | 2½ cups |
| Strong Cheddar cheese, grated | 150 g | 5 oz | 1¼ cups |
| Made English mustard | 5 ml | 1 tsp | 1 tsp |
| Snipped fresh chives | 45 ml | 3 tbsp | 3 tbsp |
| A sprig of rosemary, snipped | | | |
| Salt and freshly ground black pepper | | | |
| Egg, lightly beaten | 1 | 1 | 1 |
| Salads, to serve | | | |

① Bring a pan of water to the boil, then add the carrots and cook for about 10 minutes or until very soft. Drain and mash to a coarse purée.

② Meanwhile, heat 15 ml/1 tbsp of oil and fry (sauté) the onion and garlic until soft.

③ Combine the carrots with the onion and garlic. Mix in the breadcrumbs, cheese, mustard and herbs. Season very well, then bind the mixture with the beaten egg.

④ Place the mixture in the fridge for about 30 minutes until firm. Form into sausage shapes, then fry the sausages in a little oil for a few minutes on each side and drain on kitchen paper (paper towels).

⑤ Serve hot with a selection of salads.

PREPARATION TIME: 20 MINUTES PLUS CHILLING
COOKING TIME: 10 MINUTES

# BROCCOLI AND CAULIFLOWER KORMA

—— SERVES 4 ——

|  | METRIC | IMPERIAL | AMERICAN |
|---|---|---|---|
| Oil | 45 ml | 3 tbsp | 3 tbsp |
| Garlic cloves, finely chopped | 5 | 5 | 5 |
| Korma curry paste | 30 ml | 2 tbsp | 2 tbsp |
| Large onions, finely chopped | 2 | 2 | 2 |
| Single (light) cream | 150 ml | ¼ pt | ⅔ cup |
| Creamed coconut, cut into small pieces | 65 g | 2½ oz | 2½ oz |
| Cauliflower florets, cut into bite-sized pieces | 375 g | 12 oz | 12 oz |
| Broccoli, trimmed and cut into bite-sized pieces | 375 g | 12 oz | 12 oz |
| Finely chopped fresh coriander (cilantro) | 15 ml | 1 tbsp | 1 tbsp |
| Ground almonds | 10 ml | 2 tsp | 2 tsp |
| Garam masala | 15 ml | 1 tbsp | 1 tbsp |
| Caster (superfine) sugar | 5 ml | 1 tsp | 1 tsp |
| Salt | | | |
| Basmati rice or naan bread, to serve | | | |

① Heat the oil in a large frying pan (skillet) or wok and add the garlic. Stir-fry for about 30 seconds. Add the korma paste and keep cooking and stirring for about 1 minute.

② Add the onion and reduce the heat. Stir-fry for about 10–20 minutes so that the mixture softens and caramelises.

③ Remove the pan from the heat and liquidise the mixture in the pan using a hand blender.

④ Add the cream and coconut and stir until melted. Add the cauliflower and broccoli and simmer for 10–20 minutes until they are softened. Add a little water if necessary to prevent sticking.

⑤ Stir in the remaining ingredients, adding salt to taste, and cook, stirring constantly, for a further 5 minutes.

⑥ Serve hot with basmati rice or naan bread.

PREPARATION TIME: 20–30 MINUTES
COOKING TIME: 20–25 MINUTES

# QUICK FELAFELS
## —— SERVES 4 ——

|  | METRIC | IMPERIAL | AMERICAN |
|---|---|---|---|
| Can of chick peas (garbanzos), drained | 400 g | 14 oz | 1 large |
| Can of green lentils, drained | 400 g | 14 oz | 1 large |
| Garlic cloves | 3 | 3 | 3 |
| Ground coriander (cilantro) | 10 ml | 2 tsp | 2 tsp |
| Ground cumin | 10 ml | 2 tsp | 2 tsp |
| Chilli powder | 2.5 ml | ½ tsp | ½ tsp |
| Chopped fresh parsley | 10 ml | 2 tsp | 2 tsp |
| Onion, chopped | 1 | 1 | 1 |
| Spring onions (scallions), chopped | 4 | 4 | 4 |
| Chopped fresh coriander | 30 ml | 2 tbsp | 2 tbsp |
| Oil, for deep-frying | | | |
| Pitta bread, lemon juice or mayonnaise and Carol's Green Salad (see page 84), to serve | | | |

① Place all the ingredients apart from the oil in a processor and work to a thick paste. Leave the mixture to rest for about 30 minutes in the fridge.

② Using wet hands, form the mixture into cakes about 4 cm/1½ in across.

③ Heat the oil and deep-fry the felafels until they are golden brown. Drain on kitchen paper (paper towels) and keep warm.

④ Serve hot tucked into pitta bread pockets with a squeeze of lemon juice or mayonnaise and Carol's Green Salad.

PREPARATION TIME: 5 MINUTES PLUS CHILLING
COOKING TIME: 10 MINUTES

# CREAMY GARLIC MUSHROOM PITTA POCKETS
## —— SERVES 4

| | METRIC | IMPERIAL | AMERICAN |
|---|---|---|---|
| Butter or margarine | 10 ml | 2 tsp | 2 tsp |
| Oil | 10 ml | 2 tsp | 2 tsp |
| Garlic cloves, crushed | 2 | 2 | 2 |
| Small red onion, finely chopped | 1 | 1 | 1 |
| Button mushrooms, quartered | 225 g | 8 oz | 8 oz |
| Can of condensed mushroom soup | 300 g | 11 oz | 1 med |
| Salt and freshly ground black pepper | | | |
| Large pitta breads | 4 | 4 | 4 |
| Selection of salads, to serve | | | |

① Heat the butter or margarine and oil in a saucepan. Add the garlic and onion and fry (sauté) until softened.

② Add the mushrooms and cook until their juices start to run.

③ Stir in the condensed mushroom soup and heat through. Season to taste.

④ Split the pitta breads along one side and warm for a few minutes either under a moderate grill (broiler) or in a moderate oven.

⑤ Divide the mushroom mixture between the four pitta breads and spoon into the cavities.

⑥ Serve hot with a selection of salads.

PREPARATION TIME: 5 MINUTES
COOKING TIME: 15 MINUTES

# BALL MARROW WITH SHALLOT TOPPING

—— SERVES 4 ——

|  | METRIC | IMPERIAL | AMERICAN |
|---|---|---|---|
| Medium ball marrow (squash) | 1 | 1 | 1 |
| Extra virgin olive oil | 30 ml | 2 tbsp | 2 tbsp |
| Shallots, peeled and halved | 24 | 24 | 24 |
| Coarse sea salt and freshly ground black pepper | | | |
| Cream cheese with a black pepper coating | 175 g | 6 oz | ¾ cup |
| Pesto Potato Cakes (see page 66), to serve | | | |

① Preheat the oven to 180°C/350°F/gas mark 4.

② Cut the marrow into quarters and remove the seeds. Place the pieces skin-sides down in a roasting tin (pan) and drizzle over the olive oil. Surround with the shallots. Season well.

③ Place in the oven for about 30 minutes or until the marrow is very soft.

④ Remove the roasting tin from the oven. Take out the marrow and keep warm.

⑤ Place the roasting tin over a gentle heat and add the cream cheese. Stir until the cheese has melted.

⑥ Place the marrow quarters on warm plates, top with the shallot and cheese mixture and serve with Pesto Potato Cakes.

PREPARATION TIME: 10 MINUTES
COOKING TIME: 35 MINUTES

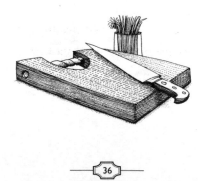

# THAI-STYLE MIXED VEGETABLES
## —— SERVES 4 ——

|  | METRIC | IMPERIAL | AMERICAN |
|---|---|---|---|
| Oil | 30 ml | 2 tbsp | 2 tbsp |
| Garlic cloves, crushed | 2 | 2 | 2 |
| Chopped fresh root ginger | 10 ml | 2 tsp | 2 tsp |
| Thinly sliced lemon grass | 15 ml | 1 tbsp | 1 tbsp |
| Hot green chillies, seeded and finely chopped | 3 | 3 | 3 |
| Medium leeks, thinly sliced | 2 | 2 | 2 |
| Spring onions (scallions), thinly sliced | 6 | 6 | 6 |
| Mangetout (snow peas), trimmed | 100 g | 4 oz | 4 oz |
| Canned baby sweetcorn (corn) cobs, drained | 12 | 12 | 12 |
| Canned coconut milk | 300 ml | ½ pt | 1¼ cups |
| Salt |  |  |  |
| Thai fish sauce | 10 ml | 2 tsp | 2 tsp |
| Lime juice | 10 ml | 2 tsp | 2 tsp |
| Chopped fresh coriander (cilantro) | 10 ml | 2 tsp | 2 tsp |
| Boiled rice, to serve |  |  |  |

① Heat the oil in a saucepan and add the garlic, ginger, lemon grass and chillies. Cook for a few minutes.

② Add the leeks and cook for about 5 minutes until they are starting to soften.

③ Stir in the spring onions, mangetout and sweetcorn and cook for a few minutes.

④ Stir in the remaining ingredients, then heat through for about 5 minutes.

⑤ Serve with plenty of hot boiled rice to mop up the juices.

PREPARATION TIME: 10 MINUTES
COOKING TIME: 15–20 MINUTES

# SAVOY MUSHROOM PARCELS
## —— SERVES 4 ——

|  | METRIC | IMPERIAL | AMERICAN |
|---|---|---|---|
| Large Savoy cabbage leaves | 8 | 8 | 8 |
| Butter or margarine | 25 g | 1 oz | 2 tbsp |
| Shallots, halved | 225 g | 8 oz | 8 oz |
| Button mushrooms, quartered | 450 g | 1 lb | 1 lb |
| Can of white wine with cream cook-in sauce | 390 g | 14 oz | 1 large |
| Salt and freshly ground black pepper |  |  |  |
| Crusty bread and Carol's Green Salad (see page 84), to serve |  |  |  |

① Preheat the oven to 190°C/375°F/gas mark 5.

② Bring a large pan of water to the boil, then blanch the whole cabbage leaves for about 4 minutes.

③ Drain well and lay out flat on a clean tea towel (dish cloth).

④ Heat the butter or margarine in a saucepan, then add the shallots and cook until softened and transparent.

⑤ Add the mushrooms and cook until the juices run.

⑥ Stir in half the can of sauce and heat through.

⑦ Divide the mixture between the cabbage leaves, spooning it on to the centre of each. Fold up the edges of each cabbage leaf to form a parcel, then place in an ovenproof dish. Pour the remaining sauce over the parcels. Cover the dish with foil.

⑧ Cook in the oven for about 25 minutes.

⑨ Serve with crusty bread and Carol's Green Salad.

PREPARATION TIME: 5 MINUTES
COOKING TIME: 25 MINUTES

# MEDITERRANEAN PICNIC LOAF
—— SERVES 4 ——

| | METRIC | IMPERIAL | AMERICAN |
|---|---|---|---|
| Medium round crusty loaf | I | I | I |
| Olive oil | 30 ml | 2 tbsp | 2 tbsp |
| Large Spanish onion | I | I | I |
| Garlic cloves, crushed | 3 | 3 | 3 |
| Small aubergine (eggplant), sliced | I | I | I |
| Medium red (bell) pepper, sliced | I | I | I |
| Medium courgette (zucchini), sliced | I | I | I |
| Chopped fresh basil | 15 ml | I tbsp | I tbsp |
| Chopped fresh oregano | 15 ml | I tbsp | I tbsp |
| Salt and freshly ground black pepper | | | |
| Mozzarella cheese, thinly sliced | 100 g | 4 oz | I cup |
| Borlotti Bean Salsa Salad (see page 90), to serve | | | |

① Slice the top off the loaf and spoon out the inside to leave the outside crusty shell. Reserve the bread for breadcrumbs.

② Heat half the oil in a frying pan (skillet) and fry (sauté) the onion and garlic until soft. Spoon into the shell.

③ Add the aubergine to the pan and fry until soft. Spoon over the onion layer.

④ Add the remaining oil to the pan and fry the pepper and courgette until tender. Place on top of the aubergine. Scatter over the herbs and season to taste. Arrange the layers of cheese all over the top, then replace the top of the loaf.

⑤ Wrap the whole filled crust tightly in clingfilm (plastic wrap), then place a plate on top and put a heavy weight on it. Leave overnight.

⑥ Remove the clingfilm, then cut the loaf into wedges and serve with a Borlotti Bean Salsa Salad.

PREPARATION TIME: 15 MINUTES
COOKING TIME: 15 MINUTES

# GNOCCHI ALLA ROMANA
## —— SERVES 2–4 ——

|  | METRIC | IMPERIAL | AMERICAN |
|---|---|---|---|
| Milk | 600 ml | 1 pt | 2½ cups |
| Salt and freshly ground black pepper | | | |
| Fine semolina (cream of wheat) | 100 g | 4 oz | ⅔ cup |
| Hard cheese, grated | 75 g | 3 oz | ¾ cup |
| Butter or margarine | 50 g | 2 oz | ¼ cup |
| Egg | 1 | 1 | 1 |
| **For the sauce:** | | | |
| Oil | 15 ml | 1 tbsp | 1 tbsp |
| Small onion, finely chopped | 1 | 1 | 1 |
| Medium red (bell) pepper, finely chopped | 1 | 1 | 1 |
| Tomatoes, skinned and chopped | 350 g | 12 oz | 12 oz |
| OR | | | |
| Can of chopped tomatoes | 410 g | 14½ oz | 1 large |
| Torn fresh basil | 15 ml | 1 tbsp | 1 tbsp |
| Chopped fresh oregano | 15 ml | 1 tbsp | 1 tbsp |
| Chopped fresh parsley (optional), to garnish | | | |
| Baby carrots and mangetout (snow peas), to serve | | | |

① Warm the milk in a saucepan with a sprinkling of salt and pepper.

② Pour in the semolina and bring to the boil, stirring constantly.

③ Reduce the heat and cook gently for 2–3 minutes until thickened.

④ Remove from the heat and add 25 g/1 oz/2 tbsp of the grated cheese and 25 g/1 oz/2 tbsp of the butter or margarine.

⑤ Beat in the egg and stir over a low heat, without boiling, for 1–2 minutes.

⑥ Turn on to a wetted plate or tray, and spread out to about 5 mm/¼ in thick. Chill until well set and cut into rounds with a small biscuit (cookie) cutter.

⑦ Arrange in overlapping rows on a buttered ovenproof dish. Sprinkle with the remaining cheese and dot with the remaining butter or margarine.

⑧ Heat under the grill (broiler), slowly at first, then more quickly to brown.

⑨ To make the sauce, heat the oil and add the onion. Fry (sauté) until transparent.

⑩ Add the pepper and fry for several minutes.

⑪ Stir in the tomatoes, basil and oregano and cook, stirring, for about 10 minutes so that the sauce thickens slightly. Season to taste.

⑫ Spoon the gnocchi on to warm plates, sprinkle with parsley and add a little of the sauce to one side. Serve with baby carrots and mangetout.

PREPARATION TIME: 20 MINUTES PLUS CHILLING
COOKING TIME: 15 MINUTES

# MUSHROOM BORLOTTI STROGANOFF
## —— SERVES 4 ——

|  | METRIC | IMPERIAL | AMERICAN |
|---|---|---|---|
| Butter or margarine | 25 g | I oz | 2 tbsp |
| Onions, sliced | 2 | 2 | 2 |
| Large garlic cloves, crushed | 2 | 2 | 2 |
| Button mushrooms, quartered | 450 g | I lb | I lb |
| Can of borlotti beans, drained | 410 g | 14½ oz | I large |
| Wholegrain mustard | 15 ml | I tbsp | I tbsp |
| White wine | 75 ml | 5 tbsp | 5 tbsp |
| Tomato purée (paste) | 10 ml | 2 tsp | 2 tsp |
| Salt and freshly ground black pepper |  |  |  |
| Soured (dairy sour) cream | 150 ml | ¼ pt | ⅔ cup |
| Chopped fresh parsley | 5 ml | I tsp | I tsp |
| Buttered noodles and Carol's Green Salad (see page 84), to serve |  |  |  |

1. Melt the butter or margarine and fry (sauté) the onion and garlic until transparent.
2. Add the mushrooms and stir until their juices start to run.
3. Stir in the beans, mustard, wine and tomato purée and boil to reduce the wine slightly.
4. Season to taste, then stir in the soured cream and warm through but do not boil. Sprinkle over the chopped parsley.
5. Serve with buttered noodles and Carol's Green Salad.

PREPARATION TIME: 5 MINUTES
COOKING TIME: 15 MINUTES

# SUNSHINE RICE
—— SERVES 4 ——

| | METRIC | IMPERIAL | AMERICAN |
|---|---|---|---|
| Brown rice, washed | 275 g | 10 oz | 2½ cups |
| Olive oil | 30 ml | 2 tbsp | 2 tbsp |
| Red onion, finely chopped | 1 | 1 | 1 |
| Hot green chillies, seeded and finely diced | 2 | 2 | 2 |
| Large red (bell) pepper, seeded and diced | 1 | 1 | 1 |
| Can of green lentils, drained | 410 g | 14½ oz | 1 large |
| Ground cumin | 5 ml | 1 tsp | 1 tsp |
| Cherry tomatoes | 16 | 16 | 16 |
| Hard-boiled (hard-cooked) eggs, quartered | 4 | 4 | 4 |
| Green olives, stuffed with pimientos | 16 | 16 | 16 |
| Salt and freshly ground black pepper | | | |
| Italian Spinach Salad (see page 91), to serve | | | |

① Place the rice in a saucepan and cover with cold water to about 1 cm/½ in above the level of the rice. Bring to the boil, stir once, then reduce the heat, cover and simmer for about 25 minutes until the rice is tender.

② Meanwhile, heat the oil and add the onion and chillies. Fry (sauté) gently until tender.

③ Add the pepper and cook for a further few minutes.

④ Stir in the lentils and cumin and heat through.

⑤ Drain the rice and add to the onion mixture.

⑥ Stir in the remaining ingredients, seasoning to taste. Heat through and serve hot with an Italian Spinach Salad.

PREPARATION TIME: 10 MINUTES
COOKING TIME: 30 MINUTES

# THREE-PEPPER LASAGNE
## —— SERVES 4 ——

|  | METRIC | IMPERIAL | AMERICAN |
|---|---|---|---|
| **For the pepper layer:** | | | |
| Oil | 30 ml | 2 tbsp | 2 tbsp |
| Onion, sliced | 1 | 1 | 1 |
| Garlic clove, crushed | 1 | 1 | 1 |
| Large red (bell) pepper, seeded and thinly sliced | 1 | 1 | 1 |
| Large green pepper, seeded and thinly sliced | 1 | 1 | 1 |
| Large yellow pepper, seeded and thinly sliced | 1 | 1 | 1 |
| Bottled passata (sieved tomatoes) | 300 ml | ½ pt | 1¼ cups |
| Dried oregano | 5 ml | 1 tsp | 1 tsp |
| Dried thyme | 2.5 ml | ½ tsp | ½ tsp |
| Dried rosemary | 2.5 ml | ½ tsp | ½ tsp |
| Salt and freshly ground black pepper | | | |
| **For the sauce layer:** | | | |
| Butter or margarine | 50 g | 2 oz | ¼ cup |
| Button mushrooms, quartered | 100 g | 4 oz | 4 oz |
| Plain (all-purpose) flour | 40 g | 1½ oz | ⅓ cup |
| Milk | 300 ml | ½ pt | 1¼ cups |
| Garlic and herb cream cheese | 100 g | 4 oz | ½ cup |
| Salt and freshly ground black pepper | | | |
| Sheets of no-need-to-precook lasagne | 9 | 9 | 9 |
| Fresh Parmesan cheese, finely grated | 50 g | 2 oz | ½ cup |
| Mixed green salad, to serve | | | |

① Preheat the oven to 190°C/375°F/gas mark 5.

② Heat the oil and add the onion and garlic. Fry (sauté) for a few minutes.

③ Add the sliced peppers and cook until they are starting to soften.

④ Stir in the passata and herbs and heat through. Season to taste and keep warm.

⑤ To make the sauce, heat the butter or margarine in a saucepan and add the mushrooms. Cook, stirring, until the mushrooms start to give out their juices.

⑥ Sprinkle in the flour and stir well. Gradually blend in the milk and bring to the boil, stirring, to give a thickened sauce.

⑦ Stir in the cream cheese until dissolved. Season to taste.

⑧ Spoon half the pepper mixture into a square or oblong ovenproof dish. Cover with three sheets of the lasagne, then spoon on half of the mushroom sauce. Cover with three sheets of the lasagne. Repeat this process, finishing with a sauce layer, then sprinkle over the Parmesan.

⑨ Place in the oven and cook for about 30–40 minutes until golden brown.

⑩ Serve hot with a simple mixed green salad.

PREPARATION TIME: 15 MINUTES
COOKING TIME: 30–40 MINUTES

# MUSTARD POTATO FRITTATA
## —— SERVES 4 ——

|  | METRIC | IMPERIAL | AMERICAN |
|---|---|---|---|
| Olive oil | 30 ml | 2 tbsp | 2 tbsp |
| Large onion, thinly sliced | I | I | I |
| Garlic clove, crushed | I | I | I |
| Button mushrooms, sliced | 4 | 4 | 4 |
| Par-boiled potatoes, sliced | 450 g | I lb | I lb |
| Dried thyme | 5 ml | I tsp | I tsp |
| Dried oregano | 5 ml | I tsp | I tsp |
| Dried rosemary | 2.5 ml | ½ tsp | ½ tsp |
| Made English mustard | 10 ml | 2 tsp | 2 tsp |
| Eggs | 4 | 4 | 4 |
| Salt and freshly ground black pepper |  |  |  |
| Garlic and Aubergine Tomatoes (see page 75), to serve |  |  |  |

① Heat the oil in a frying pan (skillet) and add the onion and garlic. Fry (sauté) until transparent.

② Add the button mushrooms and fry for a few more minutes.

③ Add the potato slices and cook, turning the potatoes frequently, for 5–10 minutes.

④ Combine the herbs with the mustard, eggs and seasoning and beat lightly. Pour the egg mixture into the frying pan and tilt the pan to distribute it evenly. Cook until the mixture is leaving the edges of the pan.

⑤ Flash the pan under a preheated grill (broiler) for several minutes so that the surface sets and browns.

⑥ Serve hot or cold with Garlic and Aubergine Tomatoes.

PREPARATION TIME: 20 MINUTES
COOKING TIME: 5–10 MINUTES

# CHEESE AND LENTIL CUTLETS
## —— SERVES 4 ——

|  | METRIC | IMPERIAL | AMERICAN |
|---|---|---|---|
| Small onion, finely chopped | 1 | 1 | 1 |
| Red lentils | 100 g | 4 oz | ⅔ cup |
| Potatoes, peeled and chopped | 450 g | 1 lb | 1 lb |
| Canned sweetcorn (corn), drained | 30 ml | 2 tbsp | 2 tbsp |
| Tomato ketchup (catsup) | 15 ml | 1 tbsp | 1 tbsp |
| Made English mustard | 10 ml | 2 tsp | 2 tsp |
| Hard cheese, grated | 100 g | 4 oz | 1 cup |
| Salt and freshly ground black pepper |  |  |  |
| Eggs, lightly beaten | 2 | 2 | 2 |
| Golden breadcrumbs | 175 g | 6 oz | 1½ cups |
| A little oil |  |  |  |
| Pieces of uncooked macaroni | 8 | 8 | 8 |
| Rustic Potatoes (see page 69) or a mixed green salad, to serve |  |  |  |

① Place the onion and lentils in a saucepan, cover with cold water and bring to the boil. Simmer for about 15–20 minutes until the lentils are soft. Drain.

② Meanwhile, boil the potatoes until very soft. Drain well and mash. Mix the sweetcorn, ketchup, mustard, cheese and seasoning into the mashed potatoes and stir in the lentil mixture.

③ Cool the mixture slightly, then form into eight cutlet shapes with your hands.

④ Dip each cutlet into the beaten egg, then coat with the breadcrumbs.

⑤ Heat a small amount of oil in a frying pan (skillet) and fry (sauté) a few cutlets at a time, turning once, until golden brown.

⑥ Insert a piece of macaroni in the end of each cutlet to resemble the bone. Serve hot with Rustic Potatoes or a mixed green salad.

PREPARATION TIME: 25–30 MINUTES
COOKING TIME: 10–15 MINUTES

# CHESTNUT AND PARSNIP TURNOVERS
## —— SERVES 4 ——

|  | METRIC | IMPERIAL | AMERICAN |
|---|---|---|---|
| Parsnip, peeled and diced | I | I | I |
| Butter or margarine | 15 ml | I tbsp | I tbsp |
| Finely grated Parmesan cheese | 15 ml | I tbsp | I tbsp |
| Frozen puff pastry (paste), thawed | 450 g | I lb | I lb |
| Unsweetened chestnut purée | 225 g | 8 oz | 8 oz |
| A pinch of grated nutmeg |  |  |  |
| Can of carrots, drained and mashed | 300 g | II oz | I med |
| Green peppercorns, roughly crushed | 10 ml | 2 tsp | 2 tsp |
| Salt |  |  |  |
| Cranberry jelly (clear conserve) | 20 ml | 4 tsp | 4 tsp |
| Egg yolk, lightly beaten | I | I | I |
| Borlotti Bean Salsa Salad (see page 90), to serve |  |  |  |

① Cover the parsnip with water and boil until tender.

② Mash the parsnip with the butter or margarine and Parmesan and allow to cool.

③ Preheat the oven to 200°C/400°F/gas mark 6.

④ Roll out the pastry and cut out four circles about 15 cm/6 in in diameter.

⑤ Combine the chestnut purée with the nutmeg and divide between the four circles, spreading almost to the edges of the pastry. Spread the carrot over the purée and the parsnip over the carrot. Sprinkle over the pepper and salt to taste. Place a teaspoon of cranberry jelly on each circle.

⑥ Brush the edges of the pastry with egg, then fold and seal the pastry over to form turnovers. Brush with egg.

⑦ Bake for 15–20 minutes until golden and puffed up.

⑧ Serve hot or cold with a Borlotti Bean Salsa Salad.

PREPARATION TIME: 15 MINUTES
COOKING TIME: 15–20 MINUTES

# CORN FRITTERS WITH SUN-DRIED TOMATO SAUCE

—— SERVES 4 ——

|  | METRIC | IMPERIAL | AMERICAN |
|---|---|---|---|
| **For the fritters:** | | | |
| Can of creamed sweetcorn (corn) | 300 g | 11 oz | 1 med |
| Plain (all-purpose) flour | 45 ml | 3 tbsp | 3 tbsp |
| Single (light) cream | 45 ml | 3 tbsp | 3 tbsp |
| Paprika | 1.5 ml | ¼ tsp | ¼ tsp |
| Salt and freshly ground black pepper | | | |
| A little oil | | | |
| **For the sauce:** | | | |
| Extra virgin olive oil | 15 ml | 1 tbsp | 1 tbsp |
| Garlic clove, crushed | 1 | 1 | 1 |
| Shallots, finely chopped | 2 | 2 | 2 |
| Sun-dried tomato purée (paste) | 60 ml | 4 tbsp | 4 tbsp |
| Italian Spinach Salad (see page 91), to serve | | | |

① Mix the creamed sweetcorn with the flour and gradually beat in the single cream. Stir in the paprika and seasoning.

② Heat about 30 ml/2 tbsp of oil in a frying pan (skillet) and drop a few spoonfuls of the mixture into the hot fat. Fry (sauté) for several minutes, then flip over and fry the other side. This is a very sticky mixture, so it is important that the fat is very hot and a spatula or fish slice with a good edge is used for turning the fritters.

③ Keep the fritters warm while frying the remainder.

④ To make the sauce: heat the olive oil in a saucepan and add the garlic and shallots and fry gently for about 5 minutes until very soft.

⑤ Stir in the tomato purée with about 60 ml/4 tbsp of water. Season the sauce to taste and heat through.

⑥ Serve the fritters hot with the sauce and an Italian Spinach Salad.

PREPARATION TIME: 10 MINUTES
COOKING TIME: 15 MINUTES

# BRUSSELS SPROUT AND CHESTNUT SOUFFLÉ
## —— SERVES 4–6 ——

|  | METRIC | IMPERIAL | AMERICAN |
|---|---|---|---|
| Butter or margarine, for greasing |  |  |  |
| Brussels sprouts, trimmed | 450 g | I lb | I lb |
| Can of chestnut purée | 439 g | 15½ oz | I large |
| Butter or margarine | 25 g | I oz | 2 tbsp |
| Plain (all-purpose) flour | 35 g | 1¼ oz | ⅓ cup |
| Milk | 300 ml | ½ pt | 1¼ cups |
| Vegetable stock cube | I | I | I |
| Cayenne | 1.5 ml | ¼ tsp | ¼ tsp |
| Grated nutmeg | 2.5 ml | ½ tsp | ½ tsp |
| Salt and freshly ground black pepper |  |  |  |
| Eggs, separated | 3 | 3 | 3 |
| Egg whites | 2 | 2 | 2 |
| Country Carrots (see page 66) and roast potatoes, to serve |  |  |  |

① Preheat the oven to 200°C/400°F/gas mark 6.

② Prepare four standard or six small ramekin dishes (custard cups): take strips of silver foil about 15 cm/6 in wide and long enough to go right round the top of the ramekin dishes and fold them in half to give a 7.5 cm/3 in depth. Wrap them around the top of the dishes to form a cuff and secure in place with tightly tied pieces of string. Use plenty of butter or margarine to grease the insides of the dishes and the foil.

③ Place the Brussels sprouts in a pan of boiling water and cook for 10–15 minutes until very soft. Cool slightly.

④ Place the drained sprouts and the chestnut purée in a food processor and process until quite smooth.

⑤ Place the butter or margarine, flour, milk, crumbled stock cube, spices and seasoning in a saucepan and beat well over a moderately high heat to make a thick, smooth sauce. Season with extra salt and pepper, if necessary. Cool slightly.

⑥    Add the sauce and the egg yolks to the sprout purée and mix very well.

⑦    Place all the egg whites in a clean mixing bowl and beat until quite stiff, then fold into the sprout mixture, using a cutting and folding action with a metal spoon.

⑧    Divide the mixture between the ramekins, piling it quite high so that it comes part of the way up the foil collars.

⑨    Place in the oven and cook for about 20 minutes or until well risen and firm on the surface but soft inside.

⑩    Serve with Country Carrots and roast potatoes.

PREPARATION TIME: 25 MINUTES

COOKING TIME: 20 MINUTES

# SPAGHETTI WITH BRIE

—— SERVES 4 ——

|  | METRIC | IMPERIAL | AMERICAN |
|---|---|---|---|
| Spaghetti | 350 g | 12 oz | 12 oz |
| Butter or margarine | 50 g | 2 oz | ¼ cup |
| Brie cheese, cut into 1 cm/½ in cubes | 150 g | 6 oz | 6 oz |
| Torn fresh basil | 15 ml | 1 tbsp | 1 tbsp |
| Salt and freshly ground black pepper |  |  |  |
| Tomato Parmesan Salad with Root Crisps (see page 93), to serve |  |  |  |

①    Bring a large pan of water to the boil, then add the spaghetti and cook for about 8 minutes until tender. Drain well.

②    Stir in the remaining ingredients, seasoning to taste.

③    Serve hot with a Tomato Parmesan Salad with Root Crisps.

PREPARATION TIME: 5 MINUTES

COOKING TIME: 8–10 MINUTES

# VEGETABLE CASSEROLE WITH TOMATO COBBLER
## —— SERVES 4 ——

|  | METRIC | IMPERIAL | AMERICAN |
|---|---|---|---|
| Onion, finely chopped | I | I | I |
| Medium carrots, thickly sliced | 2 | 2 | 2 |
| Medium parsnip, cut into<br>1 cm/½ in cubes | I | I | I |
| Large mushrooms, thickly sliced | 3 | 3 | 3 |
| Can of chopped tomatoes | 410 g | 14½ oz | I large |
| Can of mixed pulses, drained | 410 g | 14½ oz | I large |
| No-need-to-soak green lentils | 45 ml | 3 tbsp | 3 tbsp |
| Vegetable stock cube | I | I | I |
| Tomato purée (paste) | 15 ml | I tbsp | I tbsp |
| Mango chutney | 15 ml | I tbsp | I tbsp |
| Salt and freshly ground black<br>pepper |  |  |  |
| **For the cobbler:** |  |  |  |
| Wholemeal self-raising (self-rising)<br>flour | 50 g | 2 oz | ½ cup |
| White self-raising flour | 50 g | 2 oz | ½ cup |
| Salt |  |  |  |
| Butter or margarine | 25 g | I oz | 2 tbsp |
| Chopped fresh rosemary | 2.5 ml | ½ tsp | ½ tsp |
| Chopped fresh sage | 2.5 ml | ½ tsp | ½ tsp |
| Chopped fresh oregano | 2.5 ml | ½ tsp | ½ tsp |
| Cheddar cheese, grated | 25 g | I oz | ¼ cup |
| Tomato purée (paste) | 15 ml | I tbsp | I tbsp |
| Made mustard with chilli | 15 ml | I tbsp | I tbsp |
| Milk | 45 ml | 3 tbsp | 3 tbsp |
| Green vegetable, to serve |  |  |  |

① Preheat the oven to 160°C/325°F/gas mark 3.

② Place all the vegetables, the canned tomatoes and mixed pulses and the lentils into a large casserole dish (Dutch oven).

③ Stir in the crumbled stock cube, tomato purée, mango chutney and seasoning.

④    Add about 450 ml/¾ pt/2 cups of cold water. Stir well, then cover the casserole and place in the oven for about 1–1½ hours.

⑤    Meanwhile, make the cobbler topping by mixing together the flours and salt. Rub the butter or margarine into the flour until the mixture resembles breadcrumbs. Stir in the chopped herbs and grated cheese.

⑥    Combine the tomato purée with the mustard and milk. Add enough of the milk mixture to the flour mixture to make a soft dough.

⑦    Remove the casserole from the oven and increase the temperature to 200°C/400°F/gas mark 6.

⑧    Roll out the cobbler dough to about 2 cm/¾ in thick. Using a 6 cm/2½ in cutter, cut out about eight circles and arrange them on the top of the casserole.

⑨    Place in the oven and cook for about 20 minutes or until the cobbler topping is risen and brown.

⑩    Serve hot with a fresh green vegetable.

PREPARATION TIME: 15 MINUTES

COOKING TIME: 1 HOUR 50 MINUTES

# LEEK AND PEPPER LOAF WITH APPLE

—— SERVES 4 ——

|  | METRIC | IMPERIAL | AMERICAN |
|---|---|---|---|
| Large cooking (tart) apple, peeled, cored and diced | I | I | I |
| Oil, for greasing |  |  |  |
| Packet of garlic and herb stuffing mix | 160 g | 5½ oz | I small |
| Olive oil | 15 ml | I tbsp | I tbsp |
| Medium leek, thinly sliced | I | I | I |
| Small red (bell) pepper, seeded and diced | I | I | I |
| Button mushrooms, sliced | 4 | 4 | 4 |
| Salt and freshly ground black pepper |  |  |  |
| Butter or margarine | 15 g | ½ oz | I tbsp |
| Celery and Mushrooms with Boursin (see page 73) or a green salad, to serve |  |  |  |

① Preheat the oven to 200°C/400°F/gas mark 6.

② Place the apple in a saucepan with 30 ml/2 tbsp of water and slowly simmer until the apple is very soft. Mash with a fork.

③ Grease a 450 g/1 lb loaf tin (pan) and line the base with greaseproof (waxed) paper.

④ Make up the stuffing according to the packet instructions and leave to cool slightly.

⑤ Meanwhile, heat the oil and add the leeks and red pepper. Fry (sauté) gently for about 5 minutes.

⑥ Add the mushrooms and sweat for a further 5 minutes until quite soft.

⑦ Spread half the stuffing mixture evenly over the base of the loaf tin. Spread the mashed apple over the top and season. Spoon on the leek mixture and season again. Spread the remaining stuffing mixture evenly over the top. Dot the top with the butter or margarine.

⑧ Bake in the oven for 20–25 minutes until golden brown.

⑨ Allow to cool slightly before turning out and peeling off the greaseproof paper.

⑩ Serve hot or cold with Celery and Mushrooms with Boursin or a green salad.

PREPARATION TIME: 15 MINUTES
COOKING TIME: 20–25 MINUTES

# FUSILLI WITH SPINACH
—— SERVES 4 ——

|  | METRIC | IMPERIAL | AMERICAN |
|---|---|---|---|
| Fusilli | 225 g | 8 oz | 8 oz |
| Butter or margarine | 50 g | 2 oz | ¼ cup |
| Olive oil | 15 ml | 1 tbsp | 1 tbsp |
| Onion, finely chopped | 1 | 1 | 1 |
| Garlic cloves, crushed | 2 | 2 | 2 |
| Frozen chopped spinach, thawed | 100 g | 4 oz | 4 oz |
| Pine kernels, lightly toasted | 50 g | 2 oz | ½ cup |
| Salt and freshly ground black pepper | | | |
| Crisp green salad and crusty bread, to serve | | | |

① Bring a large pan of water to the boil, then add the pasta. Boil for about 8 minutes or until just tender.

② Meanwhile, heat the butter or margarine with the olive oil in a saucepan. Add the onion and garlic and fry (sauté) for a few minutes until softented.

③ Add the spinach and heat through, stirring. Add the pine kernels and season to taste.

④ Drain the pasta and stir in the spinach mixture.

⑤ Serve hot with a crisp green salad and crusty bread.

PREPARATION TIME: 5 MINUTES
COOKING TIME: 15 MINUTES

# HUMMUS AND GARLIC MUSHROOM PIE
## —— SERVES 4 ——

|  | METRIC | IMPERIAL | AMERICAN |
| --- | --- | --- | --- |
| Oil | 15 ml | I tbsp | I tbsp |
| Garlic cloves, crushed | 3 | 3 | 3 |
| Mushrooms, sliced | 350 g | 12 oz | 12 oz |
| Soy sauce | 15 ml | I tbsp | I tbsp |
| Wholemeal flour | 100 g | 4 oz | I cup |
| Plain (all-purpose) flour | 100 g | 4 oz | I cup |
| A pinch of salt |  |  |  |
| Butter or margarine | 100 g | 4 oz | ½ cup |
| Hummus | 150 g | 6 oz | ¾ cup |
| Egg, beaten | I | I | I |
| Lemon Parmesan Peas (see page 68) or a crisp green salad, to serve |  |  |  |

① Preheat the oven to 200°C/400°F/gas mark 6.

② Heat the oil in a saucepan and add the garlic and fry (sauté) for several minutes.

③ Add the mushrooms and cook for a few minutes, then stir in the soy sauce. Cook gently until the mushrooms are soft. Cool.

④ To make the pastry (paste), combine the flours and salt, then rub in the butter or margarine until the mixture resembles breadcrumbs. Stir in enough cold water to make a smooth dough.

⑤ Knead lightly, then on a floured board roll out the pastry and cut two circles to form the base and top of the pie. These should fit an 18 cm/7 in pie plate. Line the base of the plate with one piece of the pastry.

⑥ Spoon in the mushroom mixture, draining off some of the excess juice (this can be reserved and served warm with the cooked pie). Spread the hummus over the mushrooms. Brush the edges of the pastry base with a little water, then put on the pastry lid and pinch the edges to seal. Cut a small cross in the middle of the pie to let out any steam and brush the beaten egg over the pastry.

⑦ Cook in the preheated oven for about 15 minutes, then reduce the temperature to 180°C/350°F/gas mark 4 and cook for a further 15 minutes.

⑧ Serve hot or cold with Lemon Parmesan Peas or a crisp green salad.

PREPARATION TIME: 15 MINUTES
COOKING TIME: 30 MINUTES

# TAGLIATELLE WITH TOASTED NUT SAUCE
—— SERVES 4 ——

| | METRIC | IMPERIAL | AMERICAN |
|---|---|---|---|
| Walnut pieces | 50 g | 2 oz | ½ cup |
| Flaked (slivered) almonds | 75 g | 3 oz | ¾ cup |
| Oil | 5 ml | 1 tsp | 1 tsp |
| Onion, thinly sliced | 1 | 1 | 1 |
| Tagliatelle | 350 g | 12 oz | 12 oz |
| Packet of cheese sauce mix | 20 g | ¾ oz | 1 small |
| Milk, according to packet directions | | | |
| Freshly ground black pepper | | | |
| Italian Spinach Salad (see page 91), to serve | | | |

① Preheat the grill (broiler), then toast the nuts, turning to ensure that they are browned on all sides. Leave to cool, then reserve a few of the almonds for garnish.

② Heat the oil and fry (sauté) the onion until softened.

③ Cook the pasta according to the packet instructions.

④ Meanwhile, make the cheese sauce according to the packet instructions, then stir in the onion and season with pepper to taste.

⑤ Drain the cooked pasta, then stir in the sauce and toasted nuts, and garnish with the reserved almonds.

⑥ Serve hot with an Italian Spinach Salad.

PREPARATION TIME: 2 MINUTES
COOKING TIME: 20 MINUTES

# SUMMER VEGETABLE CHOW MEIN
## —— SERVES 4 ——

|  | METRIC | IMPERIAL | AMERICAN |
|---|---|---|---|
| Oil | 30 ml | 2 tbsp | 2 tbsp |
| Garlic cloves, crushed | 2 | 2 | 2 |
| French (green) beans, trimmed and cut into short lengths | 100 g | 4 oz | 4 oz |
| Mangetout (snow peas), trimmed | 100 g | 4 oz | 4 oz |
| Canned baby sweetcorn (corn) cobs, drained and cut into short lengths | 12 | 12 | 12 |
| Spring onions (scallions), finely chopped | 6 | 6 | 6 |
| Baby spinach leaves | 100 g | 4 oz | 4 oz |
| Dried egg noodles, cooked and drained | 225 g | 8 oz | 8 oz |
| Soy sauce | 10 ml | 2 tsp | 2 tsp |
| Caster (superfine) sugar | 5 ml | 1 tsp | 1 tsp |
| Vinegar | 5 ml | 1 tsp | 1 tsp |
| Sesame oil | 5 ml | 1 tsp | 1 tsp |

1. Heat a wok or large heavy-based frying pan (skillet). Pour in the oil and when hot add the garlic, beans and mangetout and cook, stirring, for several minutes until the vegetables start to soften slightly.

2. Add the sweetcorn, spring onions and spinach leaves and stir well.

3. Stir in the remaining ingredients and heat through, stirring well to ensure that the noodles do not stick.

4. Serve hot straight from the wok.

PREPARATION TIME: 10 MINUTES
COOKING TIME: 10 MINUTES

# AVOCADO AND MUSHROOM FLAN
## —— SERVES 4 ——

|  | METRIC | IMPERIAL | AMERICAN |
|---|---|---|---|
| Frozen puff pastry (paste), thawed | 350 g | 12 oz | 12 oz |
| A little flour |  |  |  |
| Garlic and herb cream cheese | 100 g | 4 oz | ½ cup |
| Onion, thinly sliced | I | I | I |
| Beef tomato, sliced | I | I | I |
| Mushrooms, sliced | 2 | 2 | 2 |
| Avocado, stoned (pitted), peeled and sliced | I | I | I |
| Olive oil | 15 ml | I tbsp | I tbsp |
| French Beans in a Zesty Lime Sauce (see page 80), to serve |  |  |  |

① Preheat the oven to 200°C/400°F/gas mark 6.

② Roll out the pastry on a floured surface to a 25 cm/ 10 in square and place on a baking (cookie) tray. Score a border about 2.5 cm/1 in inside the edge of the pastry, then prick all over the central area with a fork.

③ Spread the cheese all over the pricked area. Scatter the onion over the cheese, then arrange the tomato, mushrooms and avocado attractively on top. Brush over the surface with the olive oil.

④ Bake for about 20–25 minutes until puffed up and browned.

⑤ Serve hot or cold with French Beans in a Zesty Lime Sauce.

PREPARATION TIME: 10 MINUTES
COOKING TIME. 20–25 MINUTES

# POTATO BRUNCH TARTS

## —— SERVES 4 ——

|  | METRIC | IMPERIAL | AMERICAN |
|---|---|---|---|
| **For the pastry (paste):** | | | |
| Self-raising (self-rising) flour | 150 g | 5 oz | 1¼ cups |
| Cold mashed potato | 100 g | 4 oz | ½ cup |
| Butter or margarine, cubed | 75 g | 3 oz | ⅓ cup |
| Chopped fresh rosemary | 5 ml | 1 tsp | 1 tsp |
| Salt and freshly ground black pepper | | | |
| **For the topping:** | | | |
| Oil | 5 ml | 1 tsp | 1 tsp |
| Onion, finely chopped | 1 | 1 | 1 |
| Red (bell) pepper, seeded and diced | 1 | 1 | 1 |
| Mushrooms, thinly sliced | 100 g | 4 oz | 4 oz |
| Canned baked beans | 30 ml | 2 tbsp | 2 tbsp |
| Canned tomatoes, drained and chopped | 2 | 2 | 2 |
| Red tomato chutney or relish | 30 ml | 2 tbsp | 2 tbsp |
| Chilli powder | 2.5 ml | ½ tsp | ½ tsp |
| Eggs | 4 | 4 | 4 |
| Cheddar cheese, grated | 100 g | 4 oz | 1 cup |
| Green vegetables or Carol's Green Salad (see page 84), to serve | | | |

① Preheat the oven to 200°C/400°F/gas mark 6.

② Work the flour, potato, butter or margarine, rosemary and seasoning to a smooth dough.

③ To make the topping, heat the oil and fry (sauté) the onion and pepper for a couple of minutes. Add the mushrooms and cook until softened.

④ Stir in the beans, tomatoes, chutney and chilli and simmer for a few minutes until there is no excess liquid.

⑤ Divide the dough into four and press out into 15 cm/ 6 in circles on a baking (cookie) sheet. Press up the edges to make rough tart cases (shells).

⑥ Divide the filling between the tarts, leaving a small well in the middle of each.

⑦ Bake for 10 minutes, then break an egg into the centre of each tart and sprinkle over the grated cheese.

⑧ Return to the oven for 5 minutes until the egg is set and the pastry lightly browned.

⑨ Serve hot with green vegetables or Carol's Green Salad.

PREPARATION TIME: 15 MINUTES
COOKING TIME: 15 MINUTES

## TOMATO AND BASIL PIZZA
—— SERVES 4 ——

|  | METRIC | IMPERIAL | AMERICAN |
|---|---|---|---|
| Packet of pizza dough mix | 140 g | 5 oz | 1 |
| Dried basil | 10 ml | 2 tsp | 2 tsp |
| Sun-dried tomato purée (paste) | 30 ml | 2 tbsp | 2 tbsp |
| Spanish onion, sliced | 1 | 1 | 1 |
| Large beefsteak tomatoes, thinly sliced | 2 | 2 | 2 |
| Torn fresh basil | 30 ml | 2 tbsp | 2 tbsp |
| Salt and freshly ground black pepper | | | |
| Carol's Green Salad (see page 84), to serve | | | |

① Preheat the oven to 200°C/400°F/gas mark 6.

② Combine the pizza dough mix with the dried basil, then make the dough according to the packet instructions and leave to rest in a warm place for about 25 minutes.

③ Roll out the dough to a 20 cm/8 in circle. Spread with the tomato purée and cover with the onion and tomato. Sprinkle over the fresh basil and season to taste.

④ Bake for about 20 minutes until firm and golden.

⑤ Serve hot or cold with Carol's Green Salad.

PREPARATION TIME: 15 MINUTES PLUS RESTING
COOKING TIME: 20 MINUTES

# CHEESE AND CHUTNEY DOUGHNUTS
—— SERVES 4 ——

|  | METRIC | IMPERIAL | AMERICAN |
|---|---|---|---|
| Butter or margarine | 25 g | 1 oz | 2 tbsp |
| Thick slices of wholemeal bread | 8 | 8 | 8 |
| Very strong Cheddar cheese, grated | 100 g | 4 oz | 1 cup |
| Tangy chutney, such as apple | 60 ml | 4 tbsp | 4 tbsp |
| Self-raising (self-rising) flour | 100 g | 4 oz | 1 cup |
| Strong dry cider | 150 ml | ¼ pt | ⅔ cup |
| Salt and freshly ground black pepper |  |  |  |
| Oil, for deep-frying |  |  |  |
| Crisp green salad, to serve |  |  |  |

① Butter four slices of the bread. Divide the grated cheese between the four slices, heaping it in the middle of each slice. Top with the chutney.

② Butter the remaining bread and place butter-side up on to the other slices. Press down around the mounds of cheese and chutney to seal the edges and cut around the mounds with a sharp knife to make four round domed sandwiches.

③ Make the batter by sieving the flour, then whisking in the cider. Season.

④ Heat the oil in a deep pan to 180°C/350°F. (To test the temperature, drop in a cube of day-old bread. It should sink, then rise to the top and brown in 1 minute.)

⑤ Dip the round sandwiches in the batter, then carefully drop into the hot oil. Cook for 1–2 minutes, then flip over and cook for the same time. Remove and drain on kitchen paper.

⑥ Serve with a crisp green salad.

PREPARATION TIME: 15 MINUTES
COOKING TIME: 4 MINUTES

# ROAST ROOTS WITH FRESH HERBS

## —— SERVES 4 ——

| | METRIC | IMPERIAL | AMERICAN |
|---|---|---|---|
| Medium parsnips, peeled and cut into 6 pieces | 3 | 3 | 3 |
| Medium carrots, cut into about 6 chunks | 3 | 3 | 3 |
| Medium turnips, halved | 3 | 3 | 3 |
| Extra virgin olive oil | 45 ml | 3 tbsp | 3 tbsp |
| Onions, cut into quarters | 3 | 3 | 3 |
| Large red (bell) pepper, seeded and cut into thick strips | 1 | 1 | 1 |
| Garlic cloves, cut into slivers | 3 | 3 | 3 |
| Coarse sea salt and freshly ground black pepper | | | |
| Sprigs of fresh rosemary | 2 | 2 | 2 |
| Sprigs of fresh thyme | 2 | 2 | 2 |
| Sprig of fresh oregano | 1 | 1 | 1 |
| Green vegetable and buttered mashed potatoes, to serve | | | |

① Preheat the oven to 190°C/375°F/gas mark 5.

② Blanch the parsnip, carrot and turnip pieces in boiling water for several minutes, then drain well.

③ Place the oil in a roasting tin (pan) and heat for several minutes in the oven.

④ Place all the ingredients in the hot oil and turn well to coat, seasoning to taste. Cook in the oven for 35–45 minutes or until the vegetables are tender and tinged brown at the edges.

⑤ Serve hot with a fresh green vegetable and buttered mashed potato.

NOTE: The fresh herbs may be replaced with 1 tsp each of dried rosemary and thyme and 5 ml/½ tsp of dried oregano.

PREPARATION TIME: 15 MINUTES

COOKING TIME: 35–45 MINUTES

# SIDE DISHES

Dip into this section for some mouthwatering accompaniments to complement your main courses. Variety is your keyword here – so if your main course has a smooth texture, look for a side dish with a bit of crunch and bite or, if it looks rather bland, brighten it up with a colourful salad.

Many of the vegetable dishes in this section are substantial enough to make a complete meal in themselves, served with a salad or even another side dish.

# POTATO, SWEDE AND APPLE STRAW CAKES

—— SERVES 4 ——

|  | METRIC | IMPERIAL | AMERICAN |
|---|---|---|---|
| Medium floury potatoes, scrubbed but not peeled | 2 | 2 | 2 |
| Small swede (rutabaga), peeled and cut into large chunks | ½ | ½ | ½ |
| Crisp eating (dessert) apples, coarsely grated | 2 | 2 | 2 |
| Lemon juice | 10 ml | 2 tsp | 2 tsp |
| A pinch of grated nutmeg |  |  |  |
| Salt and freshly ground black pepper |  |  |  |
| Flour, for dusting |  |  |  |
| Oil, for brushing |  |  |  |

① Place the whole potatoes and swede pieces in a saucepan and cover with water. Bring to the boil, then simmer until both are just tender but not mushy. Drain well and cool slightly.

② Meanwhile, combine the grated apple with the lemon juice to prevent it from browning.

③ Peel the potatoes, then coarsely grate into a bowl. Grate the swede in the same way.

④ Take the grated apple in your hands and squeeze to remove all the liquid. Mix the apple into the potato and swede. Add the nutmeg and season to taste.

⑤ Form the mixture into cakes about 6 cm/2½ in across, then dust each side with flour.

⑥ Preheat the grill (broiler) to moderately hot.

⑦ Brush the cakes on one side with a little oil, then place oiled side up under the grill. Cook for 5–10 minutes until lightly browned, then flip over, brush with oil and cook the other side for a further 5–10 minutes.

⑧ Serve hot.

PREPARATION TIME: 20 MINUTES
COOKING TIME: 15–20 MINUTES

# COUNTRY CARROTS
—— SERVES 4 ——

|  | METRIC | IMPERIAL | AMERICAN |
|---|---|---|---|
| Baby new carrots, scrubbed and trimmed | 450 g | I lb | I lb |
| Butter | 15 g | ½ oz | I tbsp |
| Can of broad (fava) beans, drained | 300 g | II oz | I med |
| Packet of parsley sauce mix | 20 g | ¾ oz | I small |
| Milk, according to packet directions |  |  |  |
| Salt and freshly ground black pepper |  |  |  |
| Chopped fresh parsley | 15 ml | I tbsp | I tbsp |

① Place the carrots in a saucepan and cover with water. Bring to the boil and cook until just tender.

② Drain well, then stir in the butter or margarine and broad beans and heat through. Keep warm.

③ Make the parsley sauce according to the packet instructions, using the milk.

④ Stir the sauce into the carrots and beans and adjust the seasoning.

⑤ Serve hot sprinkled with the chopped parsley.

PREPARATION TIME: 5 MINUTES
COOKING TIME: 15 MINUTES

# PESTO POTATO CAKES
—— SERVES 4 ——

|  | METRIC | IMPERIAL | AMERICAN |
|---|---|---|---|
| Potatoes, peeled and diced | 450 g | I lb | I lb |
| Butter or margarine | 15 g | ½ oz | I tbsp |
| Pesto | 45 ml | 3 tbsp | 3 tbsp |
| Salt and freshly ground black pepper |  |  |  |
| A little oil |  |  |  |

① Bring a pan of water to the boil, then add the potatoes. Boil for 15–25 minutes until they are very soft. Drain.

② Add the butter or margarine and mash until very smooth.

③ Stir in the pesto, then season to taste.

④ Allow to cool slightly, then form into cakes about 6 cm/2½ in across. Chill for about 30 minutes.

⑤ Heat a small amount of oil in a frying pan (skillet) and fry (sauté) a few cakes at a time for about 8 minutes, turning carefully halfway through. Continue until all the cakes are cooked.

PREPARATION TIME: 30 MINUTES PLUS CHILLING
COOKING TIME: 15–20 MINUTES

# HONEYED PARSNIPS WITH MUSTARD SAUCE
—— SERVES 4 ——

|  | METRIC | IMPERIAL | AMERICAN |
|---|---|---|---|
| Large parsnips | 2 | 2 | 2 |
| Clear honey, warmed | 30 ml | 2 tbsp | 2 tbsp |
| Crème fraîche | 150 ml | ¼ pt | ⅔ cup |
| Wholegrain mustard | 15 ml | 1 tbsp | 1 tbsp |
| Salt and freshly ground black pepper |  |  |  |

① Cut the parsnips in half across the middle, then cut the bottom, thinner part into about four sticks and the top, thicker part into about eight sticks.

② Brush the parsnips with the warm honey, then place in a steamer and cover with a tight-fitting lid. Steam over boiling water for about 15 minutes or until tender. Keep warm.

③ Warm the crème fraîche and stir in the mustard. Season to taste.

④ Serve the parsnips hot on warmed plates with the sauce spooned over.

PREPARATION TIME: 5 MINUTES
COOKING TIME: 20 MINUTES

# LEMON PARMESAN PEAS

—— SERVES 4 ——

|  | METRIC | IMPERIAL | AMERICAN |
| --- | --- | --- | --- |
| Frozen peas | 450 g | I lb | I lb |
| Finely grated lemon rind | 15 ml | I tbsp | I tbsp |
| Lemon juice | 30 ml | 2 tbsp | 2 tbsp |
| Parmesan cheese, finely grated | 50 g | 2 oz | ½ cup |
| Salt and freshly ground black pepper |  |  |  |
| A twist of lemon |  |  |  |

① Cook the peas according to the packet instructions. Drain.

② Stir in the lemon rind and juice, Parmesan and seasoning.

③ Serve hot with a twist of lemon.

PREPARATION TIME: 5 MINUTES

COOKING TIME: 10 MINUTES

# ARTICHOKES IN BALSAMIC VINEGAR AND ORANGE

—— SERVES 4 ——

|  | METRIC | IMPERIAL | AMERICAN |
| --- | --- | --- | --- |
| Butter or margarine | 50 g | 2 oz | ¼ cup |
| Shallots, very finely chopped | 2 | 2 | 2 |
| Cans of artichoke hearts, drained | 2 x 400 g | 2 x 14 oz | 2 large |
| Balsamic vinegar | 30 ml | 2 tbsp | 2 tbsp |
| Fresh orange juice | 15 ml | I tbsp | I tbsp |
| Finely grated orange rind | 10 ml | 2 tsp | 2 tsp |
| Salt and freshly ground black pepper |  |  |  |

① Heat the butter or margarine and fry (sauté) the shallots until soft. Stir in the artichoke hearts and heat through.

② Add the remaining ingredients, season to taste and heat through before serving.

PREPARATION TIME: 5 MINUTES

COOKING TIME: 10 MINUTES

# RUSTIC POTATOES

—— SERVES 4 ——

|  | METRIC | IMPERIAL | AMERICAN |
|---|---|---|---|
| A knob of butter or margarine |  |  |  |
| Potatoes, peeled and sliced | 750 g | 1½ lb | 1½ lb |
| Large Spanish onion, thinly sliced | 1 | 1 | 1 |
| Black olives, stoned (pitted) and halved | 20 | 20 | 20 |
| Salt and freshly ground black pepper |  |  |  |
| Can of condensed tomato soup | 300 g | 11 oz | 1 med |
| Milk | 300 ml | ½ pt | 1¼ cups |
| Chopped fresh parsley | 15 ml | 1 tbsp | 1 tbsp |

① Preheat the oven to 190°C/375°F/gas mark 5. Use the butter or margarine to grease the inside of a fairly large casserole dish (Dutch oven).

② Place a layer of potatoes in the bottom, then a layer of onions, then sprinkle over a few olives. Season with salt and pepper. Repeat the process until the ingredients are used up, finishing with a layer of potatoes.

③ Combine the soup with the milk and pour over the contents of the casserole, allowing it to sink down. Sprinkle salt and pepper over the surface.

④ Cover the dish and place in the oven for about 40 minutes to 1 hour until the potatoes are tender.

⑤ Serve garnished with chopped parsley.

PREPARATION TIME: 10 MINUTES
COOKING TIME: 40 MINUTES–1 HOUR

# SZECHUAN CARROTS

—— SERVES 4 ——

|  | METRIC | IMPERIAL | AMERICAN |
|---|---|---|---|
| Large carrots, trimmed and peeled | 4 | 4 | 4 |
| Wholemeal flour | 60 ml | 4 tbsp | 4 tbsp |
| Szechuan peppercorns, roughly crushed | 10 ml | 2 tsp | 2 tsp |
| Grated lemon rind | 10 ml | 2 tsp | 2 tsp |
| Coarse sea salt | 2.5 ml | ½ tsp | ½ tsp |
| Oil | 15 ml | 1 tbsp | 1 tbsp |

① Preheat the oven to 190°C/375°F/gas mark 5.

② Cut the carrots in half lengthways, then cut each piece across. Cook the carrots in boiling water for 5 minutes, then drain, but keep warm in a lidded saucepan.

③ Combine the flour, peppercorns, lemon rind and sea salt on a plate. Quickly toss the carrots in the mixture so that they are coated all over.

④ Place the oil in a roasting tin (pan) and put into the oven for a few minutes until hot.

⑤ Toss the carrots in the oil, then cook in the oven for about 20 minutes, turning halfway through, to ensure that they are browned all over.

⑥ Serve hot.

PREPARATION TIME: 5 MINUTES
COOKING TIME: 20 MINUTES

# GARDEN VEGETABLES WITH PARSLEY STOCK

—— SERVES 4 ——

|  | METRIC | IMPERIAL | AMERICAN |
|---|---|---|---|
| Butter or margarine | 25 g | 1 oz | 2 tbsp |
| Shallots, finely chopped | 2 | 2 | 2 |
| Baby turnips, scrubbed and trimmed | 225 g | 8 oz | 8 oz |
| Baby carrots, scrubbed and trimmed | 225 g | 8 oz | 8 oz |
| Frozen peas | 100 g | 4 oz | 4 oz |
| Vegetable stock cube | 1 | 1 | 1 |
| Finely chopped fresh parsley | 15 ml | 1 tbsp | 1 tbsp |
| Salt and freshly ground black pepper |  |  |  |

① Heat the butter or margarine in a saucepan and gently fry (sauté) the shallots until soft.

② Add the turnips and carrots to the pan and reduce the heat. Cover and fry gently for about 5 minutes.

③ Add enough water to just cover the vegetables, then stir in the peas and stock cube and simmer for about 10 minutes until all the vegetables are quite tender.

④ Stir in the parsley, then season to taste.

⑤ Serve hot.

PREPARATION TIME: 10 MINUTES
COOKING TIME: 10 MINUTES

# BEAN AND RICE MOULDS

—— SERVES 4 ——

|  | METRIC | IMPERIAL | AMERICAN |
|---|---|---|---|
| Brown rice | 225 g | 8 oz | I cup |
| Can of mixed beans, drained | 400 g | 14 oz | I large |
| Sun-dried tomatoes, roughly chopped | 100 g | 4 oz | 4 oz |
| Tomato purée (paste) | 15 ml | I tbsp | I tbsp |
| Clear honey | 5 ml | I tsp | I tsp |
| Balsamic vinegar | 5 ml | I tsp | I tsp |
| Salt and freshly ground black pepper | | | |

① Cook the rice in a large pan of boiling, salted water, then drain, rinse in fresh boiling water and drain again.

② Stir in the remaining ingredients.

③ Divide the mixture between four ramekins (custard cups) and press down well with the back of a metal spoon.

④ Turn out immediately and serve hot as an accompaniment.

PREPARATION TIME: 5 MINUTES

COOKING TIME: 25 MINUTES

# JUNIPER CREAM CABBAGE

—— SERVES 4 ——

|  | METRIC | IMPERIAL | AMERICAN |
|---|---|---|---|
| Butter or margarine | 75 g | 3 oz | ⅓ cup |
| Firm green cabbage, very finely shredded | 350 g | 12 oz | 12 oz |
| Juniper berries, roughly crushed | 30 | 30 | 30 |
| Green peppercorns, roughly crushed | 10 | 10 | 10 |
| Single (light) cream | 150 ml | ¼ pt | ⅔ cup |
| Salt | | | |

① Heat the butter or margarine in a saucepan and add the cabbage. Stir for several minutes.

② Add the juniper berries and peppercorns and continue to cook for 5–10 minutes, stirring constantly, so that the cabbage is quite tender.

③ Stir in the cream and reduce the heat slightly. Cover the pan and cook for a further 5 minutes. Add salt to taste.

④ Serve hot.

PREPARATION TIME: 5 MINUTES
COOKING TIME: 15 MINUTES

# CELERY AND MUSHROOMS WITH BOURSIN

—— SERVES 4 ——

|  | METRIC | IMPERIAL | AMERICAN |
|---|---|---|---|
| Oil | 30 ml | 2 tbsp | 2 tbsp |
| Small red onion, finely chopped | I | I | I |
| Head of celery, sliced | I | I | I |
| Button mushrooms, sliced | 100 g | 4 oz | 4 oz |
| Boursin garlic and herb cream cheese | 150 g | 5 oz | ⅔ cup |
| Vegetable stock | 120 ml | 4 fl oz | ½ cup |
| Salt and freshly ground black pepper |  |  |  |

① Heat the oil in a saucepan and add the onion and celery. Fry (sauté) gently for about 10 minutes until they are both quite tender.

② Add the mushrooms and cook for a further 5 minutes.

③ Stir in the cheese, then blend in the vegetable stock. Season to taste and heat through.

④ Serve hot.

PREPARATION TIME: 10 MINUTES
COOKING TIME: 15 MINUTES

# CITRUS ONION MARMALADE
—— SERVES 4 ——

|  | METRIC | IMPERIAL | AMERICAN |
|---|---|---|---|
| Extra virgin olive oil | 15 ml | 1 tbsp | 1 tbsp |
| Large onions, thinly sliced | 3 | 3 | 3 |
| Dry white wine | 150 ml | ¼ pt | ⅔ cup |
| Orange juice | 45 ml | 3 tbsp | 3 tbsp |
| Lemon juice | 15 ml | 1 tbsp | 1 tbsp |
| Finely grated orange rind | 15 ml | 1 tbsp | 1 tbsp |
| Finely grated lemon rind | 5 ml | 1 tsp | 1 tsp |
| Soft brown sugar | 30 ml | 2 tbsp | 2 tbsp |
| Salt and freshly ground black pepper |  |  |  |

① Place the oil in a saucepan and, when hot, add the onions and cook until soft.

② Add the remaining ingredients and bring to the boil, stirring.

③ Reduce the heat so that the mixture is just simmering. Cover and cook gently for about 1 hour until most of the liquid has evaporated.

④ Serve hot.

PREPARATION TIME: 10 MINUTES
COOKING TIME: 1 HOUR

# GARLIC AND AUBERGINE TOMATOES

#### —— SERVES 4 ——

|  | METRIC | IMPERIAL | AMERICAN |
|---|---|---|---|
| Tomatoes | 8 | 8 | 8 |
| Extra virgin olive oil | 15 ml | 1 tbsp | 1 tbsp |
| Small onion, finely chopped | 1 | 1 | 1 |
| Garlic clove, crushed | 1 | 1 | 1 |
| Small aubergine (eggplant), finely chopped | 1 | 1 | 1 |
| Medium curry paste | 5 ml | 1 tsp | 1 tsp |
| Fresh wholemeal breadcrumbs | 60 ml | 4 tbsp | 4 tbsp |
| Salt and freshly ground black pepper |  |  |  |

① Preheat the oven to 190°C/375°F/gas mark 5.

② Halve the tomatoes, then scoop out and finely chop the flesh. Place the tomato shells in a shallow ovenproof dish.

③ Heat the oil in a pan and add the onion, garlic and aubergine. Cover the pan and sweat over a very low heat until tender.

④ Add the chopped tomato flesh and cook until soft.

⑤ Stir in the curry paste and then the breadcrumbs. Season to taste.

⑥ Pile the mixture into the tomato shells.

⑦ Cover the dish with foil and place in the oven for about 15 minutes. Remove the foil and cook for a further 10 minutes.

⑧ Serve hot.

PREPARATION TIME: 15 MINUTES
COOKING TIME: 25 MINUTES

# BEANY DROP SCONES
## —— MAKES 8–10 ——

| | METRIC | IMPERIAL | AMERICAN |
|---|---|---|---|
| Self-raising (self-rising) flour | 225 g | 8 oz | 2 cups |
| A pinch of salt | | | |
| Egg | I | I | I |
| Milk | 300 ml | ½ pt | I¼ cups |
| Can of baked beans | 420 g | 14½ oz | I large |
| A little oil | | | |
| Butter or cream cheese, to serve | | | |

① Sift the flour and salt into a large mixing bowl. Add the egg and beat in enough of the milk to make a smooth batter.

② Stir in the beans and add enough of the remaining milk to give a dropping consistency just a little thicker than double cream, then beat well.

③ Heat the oil in a large frying pan (skillet).

④ Drop a few tablespoonfuls of the mixture into the pan to form small flat cakes and cook until bubbles start to appear on the surface.

⑤ Flip the cakes over and cook for another minute or so. Remove from the pan and keep warm. Continue this process until the mixture is used up.

⑥ Serve spread with butter or cream cheese.

PREPARATION TIME: 5 MINUTES
COOKING TIME: 15 MINUTES

# CRUNCHY CURRIED PARSNIPS

—— SERVES 4 ——

|  | METRIC | IMPERIAL | AMERICAN |
|---|---|---|---|
| Large parsnips, peeled and trimmed | 2 | 2 | 2 |
| Plain (all-purpose) flour | 60 ml | 4 tbsp | 4 tbsp |
| Medium curry powder | 15 ml | 1 tbsp | 1 tbsp |
| Salt and freshly ground black pepper | | | |
| Oil | 30 ml | 2 tbsp | 2 tbsp |

① Preheat the oven to 200°C/400°F/gas mark 6.

② Cut the parsnips in half across the middle, then cut the bottom, thinner part into four sticks and the top, thicker part into eight. Place the parsnip pieces in a pan of boiling water and simmer for about 5 minutes until just tender, then drain off the water.

③ Combine the flour, curry powder and seasoning on a plate.

④ While the parsnips are still hot and damp, toss them in the flour mixture until thoroughly coated.

⑤ Pour the oil into a roasting tin (pan) and put into the oven for a few minutes until very hot.

⑥ Toss the coated parsnips in the oil and cook in the oven for about 15 minutes.

⑦ Turn the parsnips over and cook for a further 15 minutes until they are golden brown on all sides.

⑧ Serve hot.

PREPARATION TIME: 10 MINUTES

COOKING TIME: 30 MINUTES

# CARROT AND SPINACH MOULDS

—— SERVES 6 ——

|  | METRIC | IMPERIAL | AMERICAN |
|---|---|---|---|
| Carrots, peeled and cut into chunks | 450 g | I lb | I lb |
| Spinach leaves | 36 | 36 | 36 |
| Butter or margarine | 50 g | 2 oz | ¼ cup |
| Plain (all-purpose) flour | 50 g | 2 oz | ½ cup |
| Milk | 300 ml | ½ pt | I¼ cups |
| Egg | I | I | I |
| Snipped fresh chives | 15 ml | I tbsp | I tbsp |
| A pinch of grated nutmeg | | | |
| Salt and freshly ground black pepper | | | |

① Preheat the oven to 190°C/375°F/gas mark 5.

② Place the carrots in a saucepan, cover and simmer for 10–15 minutes until very soft.

③ Quickly dip each spinach leaf into a pan of boiling water to blanch and use to line the bases and sides of six ramekins (custard cups) – about six leaves to each dish.

④ When the carrots are cooked, drain and mash them into a smooth purée.

⑤ Melt the butter or margarine in a pan, add the flour and cook for 2 minutes, stirring until smooth. Gradually add the milk and simmer for 2 minutes, stirring, to make a smooth thick sauce.

⑥ Separate the egg and beat the yolk into the sauce. Whisk the egg white in a bowl until soft peaks form.

⑦ Mix the sauce and carrot together, add the chives, nutmeg and seasoning. Fold in the egg white.

⑧ Divide the mixture between the lined ramekin dishes. Place the dishes into a deep roasting tin (pan), half-filled with hot water.

⑨ Bake for 50 minutes until golden and puffed up. Turn out and serve hot.

PREPARATION TIME: 20 MINUTES

COOKING TIME: 50 MINUTES

# SQUEAKY CAKES
—— SERVES 4 ——

|  | METRIC | IMPERIAL | AMERICAN |
|---|---|---|---|
| Oil | 15 ml | 1 tbsp | 1 tbsp |
| Onion, finely chopped | 1 | 1 | 1 |
| Boiled potatoes, cooled and mashed | 450 g | 1 lb | 1 lb |
| Cooked Brussels sprouts or cabbage, cooled and finely chopped | 225 g | 8 oz | 8 oz |
| Salt and freshly ground black pepper | | | |
| A pinch of ground mace | | | |
| A little extra oil | | | |

①   Heat the oil and fry (sauté) the onion until tender.

②   Combine the onion with the mashed potatoes, Brussels sprouts or cabbage and season to taste. Stir in the mace.

③   Using slightly damp hands, form the mixture into cakes.

④   Heat the oil in a frying pan (skillet) and fry the cakes a few at a time for about 8–12 minutes, turning halfway through cooking.

⑤   Serve hot.

PREPARATION TIME: 5 MINUTES
COOKING TIME: 25 MINUTES

# FRENCH BEANS IN A ZESTY LIME SAUCE

—— SERVES 4 ——

|  | METRIC | IMPERIAL | AMERICAN |
|---|---|---|---|
| French (green) beans, trimmed | 450 g | 1 lb | 1 lb |
| **For the sauce:** | | | |
| Egg yolks | 3 | 3 | 3 |
| Finely grated lime rind | 15 ml | 1 tbsp | 1 tbsp |
| Salt and freshly ground black pepper | | | |
| Butter or margarine | 175 g | 6 oz | ¾ cup |
| Lime juice | 15 ml | 1 tbsp | 1 tbsp |
| A twist of lime | | | |

① Cover the beans with water and bring to the boil. Cook for 5–10 minutes until tender, then drain.

② Meanwhile, make the sauce. Place the egg yolks in a liquidiser with the lime rind, salt and pepper and briefly blend.

③ Heat the butter or margarine until melted and when it starts to boil pour it into a jug.

④ Turn on the liquidiser and gradually pour in the butter or margarine in a thin stream and blend until the sauce is thickened. Slowly add the lime juice in the same way.

⑤ Serve the beans with the sauce poured around and decorated with a twist of lime.

PREPARATION TIME: 5 MINUTES
COOKING TIME: 10 MINUTES

# ARTICHOKES WITH SAVOURY BUTTER

—— SERVES 4 ——

| | METRIC | IMPERIAL | AMERICAN |
|---|---|---|---|
| Butter or margarine, softened | 175 g | 6 oz | ¾ cup |
| Lemon juice | 5 ml | 1 tsp | 1 tsp |
| Snipped fresh chives | 10 ml | 2 tsp | 2 tsp |
| Chopped fresh tarragon | 2.5 ml | ½ tsp | ½ tsp |
| Tomato purée (paste) | 5 ml | 1 tsp | 1 tsp |
| Made English mustard | 1.5 ml | ¼ tsp | ¼ tsp |
| Salt and freshly ground black pepper | | | |
| Jerusalem artichokes, scraped and cut into thick slices | 450 g | 1 lb | 1 lb |

1. Combine the butter or margarine with all the ingredients except the artichokes, seasoning to taste.

2. Mix well, then form into a short sausage on a piece of clingfilm (plastic wrap) or foil. Roll up and chill until firm.

3. Cook the artichoke slices for about 10 minutes in boiling salted water until tender. Drain and keep warm.

4. Cut the flavoured butter or margarine into eight medallions.

5. Divide the artichokes between four individual bowls and place two of the medallions on the top of each so that they melt over the artichokes.

PREPARATION TIME: 15 MINUTES PLUS CHILLING
COOKING TIME: 10 MINUTES

# SALADS

I adore salads – they add colour, texture and variety to every kind of dish and, of course, they're packed full of healthy vitamins and minerals.

In this section I have included some of my favourite combinations to give you some ideas to start you off; but with the huge range of exotic fruit and vegetables now available all the year round, I'm sure you will soon be inventing your own recipes.

# MANGO AND NOODLE SALAD
#### —— SERVES 4 ——

|  | METRIC | IMPERIAL | AMERICAN |
|---|---|---|---|
| Can of mango slices, drained | 410 g | 14½ oz | I large |
| Medium egg noodles, cooked, cooled and drained | 350 g | 12 oz | 12 oz |
| Canned baby sweetcorn (corn) cobs, drained and cut into short lengths | 8 | 8 | 8 |
| Mayonnaise | 75 ml | 5 tbsp | 5 tbsp |
| Tomato ketchup (catsup) | 10 ml | 2 tsp | 2 tsp |
| Mild curry paste | 15 ml | I tbsp | I tbsp |
| Small onion, roughly chopped | I | I | I |
| Garlic clove | I | I | I |
| Salt and freshly ground black pepper |  |  |  |
| A pinch of sugar |  |  |  |

① Dice half the mango slices and combine them with the noodles and baby sweetcorn.

② Put all the remaining ingredients in a food processor or liquidiser and work to a smooth consistency.

③ Stir into the noodle mixture and serve as a main course, with a green salad or crisp vegetables.

PREPARATION TIME: 10 MINUTES

# CAROL'S GREEN SALAD
—— SERVES 4 ——

| | METRIC | IMPERIAL | AMERICAN |
|---|---|---|---|
| French (green) beans, trimmed and cut into short lengths | 16 | 16 | 16 |
| Crisp green lettuce leaves, torn | 12 | 12 | 12 |
| Spring onions (scallions), chopped | 8 | 8 | 8 |
| Large green (bell) pepper, seeded and cut into fine strips | 1 | 1 | 1 |
| Small courgettes (zucchini), cut into short sticks | 2 | 2 | 2 |
| *For the dressing:* | | | |
| Extra virgin olive oil | 45 ml | 3 tbsp | 3 tbsp |
| Lemon juice | 30 ml | 2 tbsp | 2 tbsp |
| Clear honey | 15 ml | 1 tbsp | 1 tbsp |
| Sesame seeds | 15 ml | 1 tbsp | 1 tbsp |
| Salt and freshly ground black pepper | | | |

① Blanch the French beans in boiling water for about 45 seconds.

② Mix the beans and all the salad ingredients together in a salad bowl.

③ Place all the dressing ingredients together in a screw-topped jar and shake well. Pour over the salad and toss thoroughly.

NOTE: This salad goes particularly well with any pasta dish.

PREPARATION TIME: 15 MINUTES

# FRESH HERB POTATO SALAD

## —— SERVES 4 ——

|  | METRIC | IMPERIAL | AMERICAN |
|---|---|---|---|
| Vegetable oil | 175 ml | 6 fl oz | ¾ cup |
| Egg | I | I | I |
| Dijon mustard | 10 ml | 2 tsp | 2 tsp |
| A pinch of salt |  |  |  |
| Freshly ground black pepper |  |  |  |
| A pinch of sugar |  |  |  |
| Finely chopped fresh dill | 15 ml | I tbsp | I tbsp |
| Finely chopped fresh rosemary | 5 ml | I tsp | I tsp |
| Finely chopped fresh basil | 10 ml | 2 tsp | 2 tsp |
| Finely chopped fresh oregano | 15 ml | I tbsp | I tbsp |
| Red wine vinegar | 5 ml | I tsp | I tsp |
| Lemon juice | 5 ml | I tsp | I tsp |
| Onion, thinly sliced | I | I | I |
| New potatoes, unpeeled, cooked, and quartered | 750 g | I½ lb | I½ lb |
| Bunch of chives, snipped | ½ | ½ | ½ |

① In a food processor or blender, combine 45 ml/3 tbsp of the oil, the egg, mustard, salt, pepper, sugar, herbs, vinegar and lemon juice. Blend for about 10 seconds until the mixture is slightly thickened.

② With the machine running, slowly pour the remaining oil through the feed tube in a thin, steady stream to give a thick dressing.

③ Mix the sliced onion into the potatoes and then fold in the dressing. Cover and chill.

④ Serve sprinkled with the snipped chives.

PREPARATION TIME: 10 MINUTES

# BEANSPROUT AND NUT SALAD
#### —— SERVES 4 ——

|  | METRIC | IMPERIAL | AMERICAN |
|---|---|---|---|
| Beansprouts, washed | 75 g | 3 oz | 1½ cups |
| Nectarine, stoned (pitted) and cut into small cubes | I | I | I |
| Hazelnuts (filberts), roughly chopped | 25 g | I oz | ¼ cup |
| Walnuts, roughly chopped | 25 g | I oz | ¼ cup |
| Salted peanuts | 25 g | I oz | ¼ cup |
| Sesame seeds | 15 ml | I tbsp | I tbsp |
| Walnut oil | 30 ml | 2 tbsp | 2 tbsp |
| Olive oil | 15 ml | I tbsp | I tbsp |
| Balsamic vinegar | 15 ml | I tbsp | I tbsp |
| Salt and freshly ground black pepper |  |  |  |

① Combine the beansprouts with the nectarine, nuts and sesame seeds.

② Mix together the oils, vinegar and seasoning.

③ Stir the dressing into the beansprout mixture and serve.

PREPARATION TIME: 10 MINUTES

# RED LENTILS IN A SOURED CREAM DRESSING
#### —— SERVES 4 ——

|  | METRIC | IMPERIAL | AMERICAN |
|---|---|---|---|
| Red lentils | 150 g | 5 oz | ¾ cup |
| Spring onions (scallions), thinly sliced | 4 | 4 | 4 |
| Soured (dairy sour) cream | 150 ml | ¼ pt | ⅔ cup |
| Medium curry paste | 5 ml | I tsp | I tsp |
| Salt and freshly ground black pepper |  |  |  |
| Large green salad leaves | 4 | 4 | 4 |
| Flaked (slivered) almonds, toasted | 25 g | I oz | ¼ cup |

① Cook the lentils in boiling water for about 10 minutes or until just tender. Drain and rinse in cold water.

② Stir in the spring onions. Mix in the soured cream, curry paste and seasoning.

③ Serve the lentil salad piled into the salad leaves and sprinkled with the toasted almonds.

PREPARATION TIME: 5 MINUTES
COOKING TIME: 10 MINUTES

# CRUNCHY CAMEMBERT SALAD
—— SERVES 4 ——

|  | METRIC | IMPERIAL | AMERICAN |
|---|---|---|---|
| Pasta bows, cooked and cooled | 225 g | 8 oz | 8 oz |
| Celery sticks, sliced | 2 | 2 | 2 |
| Small red onion, thinly sliced | 1 | 1 | 1 |
| Walnut pieces | 50 g | 2 oz | ¼ cup |
| Camembert cheese, cut into 1 cm/½ in cubes | 100 g | 4 oz | 1 cup |
| Mayonnaise | 30 ml | 2 tbsp | 2 tbsp |
| Soured (dairy sour) cream | 90 ml | 6 tbsp | 6 tbsp |
| Salt and freshly ground black pepper |  |  |  |
| Snipped fresh chives | 30 ml | 2 tbsp | 2 tbsp |

① Combine the pasta, celery, onion, walnuts and cheese.

② Fold in the mayonnaise and soured cream and season to taste.

③ Serve the salad in individual bowls sprinkled with the snipped chives.

PREPARATION TIME: 10 MINUTES

# WARM GINGERED TOFU SALAD

—— SERVES 4 ——

|  | METRIC | IMPERIAL | AMERICAN |
|---|---|---|---|
| Oil | 15 ml | 1 tbsp | 1 tbsp |
| Piece of fresh root ginger, peeled and finely chopped | 2.5 cm | 1 in | 1 in |
| Garlic clove, crushed | 1 | 1 | 1 |
| Mangetout (snow peas), trimmed | 100 g | 4 oz | 4 oz |
| Can of baby sweetcorn (corn) cobs, drained | 250 g | 9 oz | 1 med |
| Smoked tofu, cut into 1 cm/½ in cubes | 225 g | 8 oz | 8 oz |
| A dash of soy sauce | | | |
| Salt and freshly ground black pepper | | | |

① Heat the oil, add the ginger and garlic and cook gently until softened.

② Add the mangetout and sweetcorn and toss briefly to mix.

③ Stir in the tofu and heat through.

④ Add a dash of soy sauce and season to taste.

⑤ Serve warm.

PREPARATION TIME: 5 MINUTES
COOKING TIME: 5 MINUTES

# CHINESE VEGETABLES IN PEANUT MAYONNAISE
## —— SERVES 4 ——

| | METRIC | IMPERIAL | AMERICAN |
|---|---|---|---|
| Mangetout (snow peas), blanched | 75 g | 3 oz | 3 oz |
| Can of baby sweetcorn (corn) cobs, drained and cut into short lengths | 425 g | 15 oz | 1 large |
| Spring onions (scallions), cut into short lengths | 4 | 4 | 4 |
| Radishes, thickly sliced | 4 | 4 | 4 |
| Small red (bell) pepper, seeded and thinly sliced | 1 | 1 | 1 |
| Beansprouts, washed and dried | 100 g | 4 oz | 4 oz |
| **For the peanut mayonnaise:** | | | |
| Mayonnaise | 75 ml | 5 tbsp | 5 tbsp |
| Peanut butter | 15 ml | 1 tbsp | 1 tbsp |
| Chopped fresh root ginger | 2.5 ml | ½ tsp | ½ tsp |
| A pinch of soft brown sugar | | | |
| Soy sauce | 10 ml | 2 tsp | 2 tsp |
| Chilli powder | 1.25 ml | ¼ tsp | ¼ tsp |
| Garlic clove, crushed | 1 | 1 | 1 |

① Mix the vegetables together in a salad bowl.

② Combine all the ingredients for the peanut mayonnaise and mix very well.

③ Stir the dressing into the vegetables and serve.

PREPARATION TIME: 10 MINUTES

## BORLOTTI BEAN SALSA SALAD
—— SERVES 4 ——

|  | METRIC | IMPERIAL | AMERICAN |
|---|---|---|---|
| Red onion, very finely chopped | 1 | 1 | 1 |
| Garlic cloves, very finely chopped | 2 | 2 | 2 |
| Hot green chillies, seeded and very finely chopped | 2 | 2 | 2 |
| Avocado, peeled and cut into small cubes | 1 | 1 | 1 |
| Medium red (bell) pepper, diced very finely | ½ | ½ | ½ |
| Can of borlotti beans, drained | 410 g | 14 oz | 1 large |
| Extra virgin olive oil | 45 ml | 3 tbsp | 3 tbsp |
| Freshly ground black pepper |  |  |  |
| Coarse salt |  |  |  |
| Chopped fresh coriander (cilantro) | 15 ml | 1 tbsp | 1 tbsp |

① Combine all the ingredients and stir well.

② Serve as part of a selection of salads or as an accompaniment to pastry dishes.

PREPARATION TIME: 10 MINUTES

# ITALIAN SPINACH SALAD
#### —— SERVES 4 ——

| | METRIC | IMPERIAL | AMERICAN |
|---|---|---|---|
| Baby spinach leaves, washed | 450 g | I lb | I lb |
| Spring onions (scallions), finely chopped | 5 | 5 | 5 |
| Extra virgin olive oil | 60 ml | 4 tbsp | 4 tbsp |
| Balsamic vinegar | 15 ml | I tbsp | I tbsp |
| Parmesan cheese, finely grated | 75 g | 3 oz | ⅓ cup |
| Pine kernels | 50 g | 2 oz | ½ cup |
| Salt and freshly ground black pepper | | | |

① Place the spinach leaves in a salad bowl.

② Combine all the remaining ingredients, seasoning very well, and toss with the spinach leaves so that they are coated with the dressing.

PREPARATION TIME: 5 MINUTES

# BUTTER BEAN AND TOMATO SALAD
#### —— SERVES 4 ——

| | METRIC | IMPERIAL | AMERICAN |
|---|---|---|---|
| Tomatoes, quartered | 4 | 4 | 4 |
| Can of butter (lima) beans, drained | 300 g | II oz | I med |
| Garlic clove, crushed | I | I | I |
| Torn fresh basil | 30 ml | 2 tbsp | 2 tbsp |
| Greek yoghurt | 75 ml | 5 tbsp | 5 tbsp |
| Salt and freshly ground black pepper | | | |
| A sprig of basil, to garnish | | | |
| Warm crusty bread, to serve | | | |

① Combine all the ingredients, reserving the sprig of basil for a garnish.

② Serve chilled with warm crusty bread.

PREPARATION TIME: 5 MINUTES

# WALNUT-DRESSED COLESLAW
## —— SERVES 4 ——

|  | METRIC | IMPERIAL | AMERICAN |
|---|---|---|---|
| Small white cabbage, finely shredded | I | I | I |
| Large carrot, finely diced | I | I | I |
| Red eating (dessert) apple, cored and diced | I | I | I |
| Red onion, chopped | I | I | I |
| Walnut pieces | 50 g | 2 oz | ½ cup |
| *For the dressing:* | | | |
| Large garlic clove, crushed | I | I | I |
| Green peppercorns, crushed | 5 ml | I tsp | I tsp |
| Coarse sea salt | 5 ml | I tsp | I tsp |
| Caster (superfine) sugar | 2.5 ml | ½ tsp | ½ tsp |
| Walnut pieces | 100 g | 4 oz | I cup |
| Extra virgin olive oil | 150 ml | ¼ pt | ⅔ cup |
| Lemon juice | 30 ml | 2 tbsp | 2 tbsp |
| Chopped fresh parsley | 15 ml | I tbsp | I tbsp |

① Combine the vegetables and walnut pieces to make the coleslaw.

② Place the dressing ingredients in a liquidiser or processor and blend for a few minutes to give a smooth mixture.

③ Stir through the coleslaw and serve.

PREPARATION TIME: 15 MINUTES

# TOMATO PARMESAN SALAD WITH ROOT CRISPS
## —— SERVES 4 ——

| | METRIC | IMPERIAL | AMERICAN |
|---|---|---|---|
| Oil, for deep-frying | | | |
| Beetroot (red beet), very thinly sliced | I | I | I |
| Parsnip, peeled and very thinly sliced | I | I | I |
| Large carrot, peeled and very thinly sliced | I | I | I |
| Parmesan cheese, finely grated | 50 g | 2 oz | ½ cup |
| Extra virgin olive oil | 60 ml | 4 tbsp | 4 tbsp |
| Salt and freshly ground black pepper | | | |
| Cherry tomatoes | 450 g | I lb | I lb |
| Roughly chopped fresh coriander (cilantro) | 15 ml | I tbsp | I tbsp |

① Heat the oil in a pan suitable for deep-fat frying.

② Fry (sauté) the sliced vegetables a few at a time, for a couple of minutes, then drain on kitchen paper (paper towels). Leave to cool.

③ Combine the Parmesan cheese, olive oil and seasoning and toss the tomatoes in the mixture.

④ Serve the tomatoes topped with the root crisps and scatter the coriander over the top.

PREPARATION TIME: 10 MINUTES
COOKING TIME: 5 MINUTES

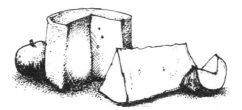

# CUCUMBER WITH DILL SOURED CREAM
## —— SERVES 4 ——

|  | METRIC | IMPERIAL | AMERICAN |
|---|---|---|---|
| Large cucumber | I | I | I |
| Soured (dairy sour) cream | 150 ml | ¼ pt | ⅔ cup |
| Chopped fresh dill (dill weed) | 15 ml | I tbsp | I tbsp |
| Green peppercorns, crushed | 5 ml | I tsp | I tsp |
| Salt |  |  |  |
| Salads and crusty bread, to serve |  |  |  |

①  Trim the ends off the cucumber, cut in half lengthways and scoop out and discard the seeds. Cut the cucumber into 1 cm/½ in cubes.

②  Combine with the remaining ingredients, season to taste and serve as an accompaniment to salads and crusty bread.

PREPARATION TIME: 10 MINUTES

# FLAGEOLET RED SALAD
## —— SERVES 4 ——

|  | METRIC | IMPERIAL | AMERICAN |
|---|---|---|---|
| Can of flageolet beans, drained | 410 g | 14½ oz | I large |
| Garlic clove, crushed | I | I | I |
| Small red onion, thinly sliced | I | I | I |
| Small red (bell) pepper, seeded and very finely diced | I | I | I |
| Ready-made red pesto | 60 ml | 4 tbsp | 4 tbsp |
| Extra virgin olive oil | 15 ml | I tbsp | I tbsp |
| Salt and freshly ground black pepper |  |  |  |
| Radicchio leaves, to garnish |  |  |  |

①  Combine all the ingredients except the radicchio.

②  Arrange the radicchio leaves on a platter, pile the flageolet salad on top and serve.

PREPARATION TIME: 5 MINUTES

# POTATO SALAD WITH HORSERADISH MAYONNAISE
#### —— SERVES 4 ——

|  | METRIC | IMPERIAL | AMERICAN |
|---|---|---|---|
| Baby salad potatoes, scrubbed and halved | 450 g | 1 lb | 1 lb |
| Olive oil | 30 ml | 2 tbsp | 2 tbsp |
| Butter or margarine | 15 ml | 1 tbsp | 1 tbsp |
| Spring onions (scallions), thinly sliced | 6 | 6 | 6 |
| Salt and freshly ground black pepper |  |  |  |
| Mayonnaise | 150 ml | ¼ pt | ⅔ cup |
| Creamed horseradish sauce | 15 ml | 1 tbsp | 1 tbsp |

① Cover the potatoes with water and bring to the boil and cook until they are just tender. Drain well.

② Heat the olive oil and butter or margarine in a frying pan (skillet) and add the potatoes. Fry (sauté) briskly so that the potatoes brown on all sides.

③ Add the spring onions and cook until they are crispy.

④ Drain on kitchen paper (paper towels) and sprinkle with the salt and pepper.

⑤ Combine the mayonnaise and horseradish sauce and season to taste.

⑥ Serve the warm potatoes with the cold mayonnaise with a selection of salads.

PREPARATION TIME: 10 MINUTES
COOKING TIME: 15 MINUTES

# DESSERTS

Sticking to a vegetarian diet doesn't mean you can't treat yourself. This section is full of delicious ways to round off your meal, and, because they are packed with nutritious ingredients like fruit, nuts and honey, you can tell yourself they are good for you, too.

# COFFEE AND TIA MARIA BOMBE
## —— SERVES 4 ——

|  | METRIC | IMPERIAL | AMERICAN |
|---|---|---|---|
| Double (heavy) or whipping cream | 300 ml | ½ pt | 1¼ cups |
| Instant coffee granules | 5 ml | 1 tsp | 1 tsp |
| Hot water | 15 ml | 1 tbsp | 1 tbsp |
| Tia Maria | 45 ml | 3 tbsp | 3 tbsp |
| Sponge (lady) fingers, broken into 4 pieces | 8 | 8 | 8 |
| Meringue shells, broken into small pieces | 75 g | 3 oz | 3 oz |
| A little oil, for greasing |  |  |  |
| Bananas | 2 | 2 | 2 |

① Whip the cream until thick.

② Combine the coffee, hot water and 30 ml/2 tbsp of the Tia Maria.

③ Quickly dip the broken sponge fingers into the coffee mixture, then gently stir into the cream. Stir in the meringue pieces.

④ Spoon the mixture into a lightly greased 600 ml/1 pt/2½ cup pudding basin and smooth the surface with the back of a tablespoon.

⑤ Cover with clingfilm (plastic wrap) and freeze for about 2 hours until firm.

⑥ Turn the bombe out on to a large serving plate and thaw for about 10 minutes in the refrigerator.

⑦ Slice the bananas, toss in the remaining Tia Maria and arrange around the bombe. Serve immediately.

NOTE: This dish can be made in a ring mould, then served with the centre filled with the sliced bananas.

PREPARATION TIME: 10 MINUTES PLUS FREEZING AND THAWING

# GOOSEBERRY OATMEAL MEDLEY
#### —— SERVES 4 ——

|  | METRIC | IMPERIAL | AMERICAN |
|---|---|---|---|
| Medium oatmeal | 50 g | 2 oz | ½ cup |
| Hazelnuts (filberts), coarsely chopped | 50 g | 2 oz | ½ cup |
| Double (heavy) cream | 150 ml | ¼ pt | ⅔ cup |
| Greek yoghurt | 150 ml | ¼ pt | ⅔ cup |
| Clear honey | 45 ml | 3 tbsp | 3 tbsp |
| Can of gooseberries, drained | 300 g | 11 oz | 1 large |
| Whole hazelnuts | 4 | 4 | 4 |

① Preheat the grill (broiler).

② Place the oatmeal and chopped hazelnuts in the grill pan (without the rack) and toast until lightly browned. Allow to cool.

③ Meanwhile, whisk the cream, yoghurt and honey together until thick.

④ Fold the oatmeal and nuts into the cream mixture with a metal spoon. Divide half the cream mixture between four sundae glasses. Top with the gooseberries. Cover the gooseberries with the remaining cream mixture. Chill.

⑤ Serve topped with the whole hazelnuts.

PREPARATION TIME: 15 MINUTES
COOKING TIME: 5 MINUTES

# QUICK PLUM AND APPLE FOOL

## —— SERVES 4 ——

|  | METRIC | IMPERIAL | AMERICAN |
|---|---|---|---|
| Large cooking (tart) apples, peeled, cored and chopped | 2 | 2 | 2 |
| Large plums | 6 | 6 | 6 |
| Soft brown sugar | 15 ml | 1 tbsp | 1 tbsp |
| Clear honey | 15 ml | 1 tbsp | 1 tbsp |
| Double (heavy) or whipping cream | 300 ml | ½ pt | 1¼ cups |
| Plain yoghurt | 150 ml | ¼ pt | ⅔ cup |
| Crisp dessert biscuits (cookies), to serve | | | |

① Place the fruit in a saucepan with a tight-fitting lid and simmer until it is very soft.

② Rub the fruit through a sieve (strainer). Return to the pan and boil for a few minutes to give a thick purée.

③ Stir in the sugar and honey. Cool.

④ Whip the cream until quite stiff, then fold in the yoghurt and fruit purée. Spoon into sundae dishes and serve cold with crisp dessert biscuits.

PREPARATION TIME: 10 MINUTES

COOKING TIME: 10 MINUTES

# BUTTERSCOTCH APPLE PANCAKES
## —— SERVES 4 ——

|  | METRIC | IMPERIAL | AMERICAN |
|---|---|---|---|
| Packet of pancake batter mixture | 130 g | 4 oz | 1 |
| Milk, according to packet directions |  |  |  |
| A little oil |  |  |  |
| Fresh breadcrumbs | 100 g | 4 oz | 2 cups |
| Butter or margarine | 75 g | 3 oz | ⅓ cup |
| Grated rind and juice of 1 lemon |  |  |  |
| Cooking (tart) apples, peeled, cored and sliced | 750 g | 1½ lb | 1½ lb |
| Caster (superfine) sugar | 50 g | 2 oz | ¼ cup |
| Ground cinnamon | 5 ml | 1 tsp | 1 tsp |
| **For the sauce:** |  |  |  |
| Butter or margarine | 50 g | 2 oz | ¼ cup |
| Dark brown sugar | 30 ml | 2 tbsp | 2 tbsp |
| Golden (light corn) syrup | 30 ml | 2 tbsp | 2 tbsp |
| Crème fraîche, to serve |  |  |  |

① Preheat the oven to 180°C/350°F/gas mark 4.

② Make up the pancake batter according to the packet instructions.

③ Heat a little oil in a frying pan (skillet) until very hot, running it round to ensure that the whole surface of the pan is coated. Pour off any surplus. Ladle in a little batter, rotating the pan at the same time, until enough batter is added to give a thin coating.

④ Cook until the pancake begins to curl around the edges, flip over with a palette knife and briefly cook the other side. Remove from the pan and keep warm.

⑤ Continue the process until all the batter is used up, adding a little oil to the pan when necessary.

⑥ Fry the breadcrumbs in 50 g/2 oz/¼ cup of the butter or margarine until golden, stirring frequently.

⑦ Place the remainder of the butter or margarine, the lemon rind and juice, apples, caster sugar and cinnamon in a saucepan. Cover and cook to a purée, then add the breadcrumbs.

⑧ Divide the mixture between the pancakes and roll up. Place in an ovenproof dish.

⑨ To make the sauce, melt the butter or margarine in a saucepan, then stir in the brown sugar and syrup. Heat, stirring, until melted.

⑩ Pour the sauce over the pancakes, cover the dish with foil and place in the oven for about 25 minutes.

⑪ Serve hot with crème fraîche.

PREPARATION TIME: 30 MINUTES
COOKING TIME: 25 MINUTES

# PINEAPPLE IN CARAMELISED COCONUT SAUCE

—— SERVES 4 ——

|  | METRIC | IMPERIAL | AMERICAN |
|---|---|---|---|
| Medium pineapple | 1 | 1 | 1 |
| OR Cans of pineapple rings, drained | 2 × 432 g | 2 × 14½ oz | 2 large |
| Double (heavy) cream | 300 ml | ½ pt | 1¼ cups |
| Creamed coconut, cut into small pieces | 100 g | 4 oz | 4 oz |
| Soft brown sugar | 75 g | 3 oz | ⅓ cup |

① If using fresh pineapple, remove the top and bottom, cut off the skin, remove the core and cut into rings 1 cm/½ in thick.

② Place the pineapple in a fairly shallow ovenproof dish.

③ Warm the cream gently in a saucepan and stir in the coconut until dissolved. Pour over the pineapple.

④ Sprinkle the sugar over the top and quickly place under a preheated grill (broiler). Cook until the sugar has caramelised. Serve piping hot.

PREPARATION TIME: 10 MINUTES
COOKING TIME: 5 MINUTES

# SWISS RASPBERRY LAYERS
## —— SERVES 4 ——

|  | METRIC | IMPERIAL | AMERICAN |
|---|---|---|---|
| Slices of chocolate Swiss (jelly) roll | 8 | 8 | 8 |
| Melted butter or margarine | 15 ml | 1 tbsp | 1 tbsp |
| Golden (light corn) syrup, slightly warmed | 15 ml | 1 tbsp | 1 tbsp |
| Cocoa (unsweetened chocolate) powder | 10 ml | 2 tsp | 2 tsp |
| Raspberries, fresh or thawed frozen | 225 g | 8 oz | 8 oz |
| Can of ready-made custard | 400 g | 14 oz | 1 large |
| Whipping cream | 150 ml | ¼ pt | ⅔ cup |
| Plain (semi-sweet) chocolate, finely grated | 25 g | 1 oz | ¼ cup |

① Place the Swiss roll, the butter or margarine, golden syrup and cocoa in a liquidiser or food processor and blend until smooth.

② Divide the mixture between four sundae glasses and cool slightly.

③ Reserve four raspberries, then pile the rest on to the chocolate layer in the glasses.

④ Divide the custard between the glasses and cover the raspberry layer. Whip the cream and spread over the custard. Chill.

⑤ Decorate with the grated chocolate and the reserved raspberries.

PREPARATION TIME: 20 MINUTES

# LAYERED RHUBARB CRISP WITH GINGERED CREAM

—— SERVES 4 ——

|  | METRIC | IMPERIAL | AMERICAN |
|---|---|---|---|
| **For the base:** | | | |
| Chocolate digestive biscuits (Graham crackers) | 100 g | 4 oz | 4 oz |
| Ginger nuts | 100 g | 4 oz | 4 oz |
| Butter or margarine | 100 g | 4 oz | 4 oz |
| **For the filling:** | | | |
| Rhubarb, sliced | 450 g | 1 lb | 1 lb |
| Soft brown sugar | 25 g | 1 oz | 2 tbsp |
| **For the topping:** | | | |
| Double (heavy) cream | 150 ml | ¼ pt | ⅔ cup |
| Greek yoghurt | 150 ml | ¼ pt | ⅔ cup |
| Ground ginger | 2.5 ml | ½ tsp | ½ tsp |
| Butter or margarine | 15 g | ½ oz | 1 tbsp |
| Golden (light corn) syrup | 15 ml | 1 tbsp | 1 tbsp |
| Soft brown sugar | 15 ml | 1 tbsp | 1 tbsp |
| Cornflakes | 75 g | 3 oz | 1½ cups |

① To make the base, grind all the biscuits (cookies) into fine crumbs in a food processor.

② Melt the butter or margarine and stir into the biscuit crumbs. Press the mixture into a 20 cm/8 in loose-bottomed flan tin (pie pan). Chill to set.

③ To make the filling, place the rhubarb in a saucepan with the sugar and 15 ml/1 tbsp of water. Simmer gently until the rhubarb is soft and pulpy.

④ Allow to cool, then spread over the biscuit base.

⑤ For the topping, whisk the cream, yoghurt and ginger together until the mixture is thick and forms peaks. Pile over the rhubarb layer and chill.

⑥ Melt the butter or margarine, syrup and sugar in a pan, then stir in the cornflakes, until well coated.

⑦ Allow the mixture to cool completely and become crispy, then spoon all over the cream layer. Serve chilled.

PREPARATION TIME: 30 MINUTES

# HONEY PEACH YOGHURT ICE

—— SERVES 4–6 ——

| | METRIC | IMPERIAL | AMERICAN |
|---|---|---|---|
| Cans of peach slices, drained | 2 × 410 g | 2 × 14½ oz | 2 large |
| Lemon juice | 30 ml | 2 tbsp | 2 tbsp |
| Clear honey | 45 ml | 3 tbsp | 3 tbsp |
| Ground cinnamon | 5 ml | 1 tsp | 1 tsp |
| Plain yoghurt | 225 g | 8 oz | 2 cups |
| Caster (superfine) sugar | 175 g | 6 oz | ¾ cup |
| Quark | 225 g | 8 oz | 1 cup |
| Langue de chat biscuits (cookies), to serve | | | |

1. Place the peach slices, lemon juice, honey and cinnamon in a liquidiser and blend until smooth.
2. Whisk the yoghurt and the sugar together, then mix with the fruit purée.
3. Beat the quark until smooth, then fold into the peach mixture with a metal spoon.
4. Place in a suitable container, then place in the freezer until the mixture is just starting to freeze around the edges.
5. Turn out into a mixing bowl and beat well to reduce the size of the ice crystals forming and prevent too hard a texture. Return to the freezer and freeze until solid.
6. Remove from the freezer about 1 hour before serving and leave in a cool place to soften slightly, then serve scoops in sundae glasses with langue de chat biscuits.

PREPARATION TIME: 15 MINUTES PLUS FREEZING

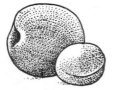

# MULLED CHERRIES WITH CINNAMON

—— SERVES 4 ——

| | METRIC | IMPERIAL | AMERICAN |
|---|---|---|---|
| Cans of stoned (pitted) black cherries | 2 × 410 g | 2 × 14½ oz | 2 large |
| Cloves | 6 | 6 | 6 |
| Orange | ½ | ½ | ½ |
| Lemon | ½ | ½ | ½ |
| Cinnamon stick | 1 | 1 | 1 |
| Grated nutmeg | 1.5 ml | ¼ tsp | ¼ tsp |
| Soft brown sugar | 30 ml | 2 tbsp | 2 tbsp |
| Red wine | 450 ml | ¾ pt | 2 cups |
| Ground cinnamon | 5 ml | 1 tsp | 1 tsp |
| Crème fraîche | 150 ml | ¼ pt | ⅔ cup |

① Empty the cherries with their syrup into a fairly large saucepan.

② Stick the cloves into the skin of the orange and place in the saucepan. Add the lemon, cinnamon stick, nutmeg, brown sugar and red wine.

③ Bring slowly to the boil, then reduce the heat and simmer gently for about 10 minutes or until the liquid is slightly reduced. Remove the orange, lemon and cinnamon stick.

④ Combine the ground cinnamon with the crème fraîche.

⑤ Ladle the cherries into warm bowls and serve topped with spoonfuls of the cold cinnamon crème fraîche.

PREPARATION TIME: 5 MINUTES
COOKING TIME: 10 MINUTES

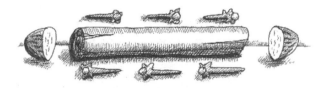

# MIDDLE EASTERN DREAM DESSERT

—— SERVES 4 ——

| | METRIC | IMPERIAL | AMERICAN |
|---|---|---|---|
| Ground rice | 50 g | 2 oz | ½ cup |
| Cornflour (cornstarch) | 25 g | 1 oz | ¼ cup |
| Fresh orange juice | 30 ml | 2 tbsp | 2 tbsp |
| Milk | 900 ml | 1½ pts | 3¾ cups |
| Cardamom pods, slightly crushed | 6 | 6 | 6 |
| Cloves | 6 | 6 | 6 |
| Piece of cinnamon stick | 5 cm | 2 in | 2 in |
| Single (light) cream | 150 ml | ¼ pt | ⅔ cup |
| Soft brown sugar | 75 g | 3 oz | ⅓ cup |
| Finely grated orange rind | 15 ml | 1 tbsp | 1 tbsp |
| Ground almonds | 50 g | 2 oz | ½ cup |
| Flaked (slivered) almonds, lightly toasted | 50 g | 2 oz | ½ cup |
| Cream or Greek yoghurt, to serve | | | |

① Blend together the rice and cornflour with the orange juice to give a smooth paste.

② Place the milk in a saucepan with the spices and gradually bring to the boil. Reduce the heat slightly and simmer gently for several minutes. Strain the spices off from the milk.

③ Stir the blended rice mixture into the hot milk and return to the heat. Cook, stirring constantly, until the mixture is slightly thickened.

④ Remove from the heat and stir in the cream, sugar, orange rind and ground almonds.

⑤ Pour into glass sundae dishes and chill.

⑥ Serve decorated with the toasted almonds with either extra cream or Greek yoghurt.

PREPARATION TIME: 10 MINUTES
COOKING TIME: 10 MINUTES

# CHOCOLATE CHESTNUT CASTLES

—— SERVES 4 ——

| | METRIC | IMPERIAL | AMERICAN |
|---|---|---|---|
| Oil, for greasing | | | |
| Plain (semi-sweet) chocolate, broken into pieces | 150 g | 5 oz | 1¼ cups |
| Butter or margarine | 50 g | 2 oz | ¼ cup |
| Soft brown sugar | 50 g | 2 oz | ¼ cup |
| Can of unsweetened chestnut purée | 439 g | 15½ oz | 1 large |
| Cointreau | 15 ml | 1 tbsp | 1 tbsp |
| Ratafia biscuits (cookies), crushed roughly | 50 g | 2 oz | 2 oz |
| Double (heavy) cream, whipped | 150 ml | ¼ pt | ⅔ cup |
| Cocoa (unsweetened chocolate) powder | 5 ml | 1 tsp | 1 tsp |

① Oil four dariole moulds, then line with clingfilm (plastic wrap), ensuring that the surface is smooth. Brush the clingfilm lightly with a little more oil.

② Place the chocolate in a saucepan with 30 ml/2 tbsp of water and heat gently until the chocolate has melted. Cool.

③ Beat together the butter or margarine, sugar and chestnut purée or blend together in a processor, if you prefer. Add the chocolate and Cointreau and mix thoroughly. Stir through the crushed ratafia biscuits.

④ Divide the mixture between the dariole moulds. Smooth the surface and chill for several hours.

⑤ Invert the dariole moulds and turn the castles out on to individual serving plates, peeling off the clingfilm. Pipe a large swirl of cream on to the top of each castle and sift a little cocoa powder over the top.

PREPARATION TIME: 15 MINUTES

COOKING TIME: 5 MINUTES

# MIXED BERRY BRÛLÉE
—— SERVES 4 ——

|  | METRIC | IMPERIAL | AMERICAN |
|---|---|---|---|
| Strawberries, hulled | 225 g | 8 oz | 8 oz |
| Fresh or thawed frozen raspberries, hulled | 225 g | 8 oz | 8 oz |
| Blackberries | 225 g | 8 oz | 8 oz |
| Blueberries | 225 g | 8 oz | 8 oz |
| Port | 30 ml | 2 tbsp | 2 tbsp |
| Soft brown sugar | 45 ml | 3 tbsp | 3 tbsp |
| Double (heavy) cream | 150 ml | ¼ pt | ⅔ cup |
| Greek yoghurt | 150 ml | ¼ pt | ⅔ cup |
| A few drops of vanilla essence (extract) | | | |
| Caster (superfine) sugar | 60 ml | 4 tbsp | 4 tbsp |
| Langue de chat biscuits (cookies), to serve | | | |

① Place the fruit in a saucepan with the port and brown sugar. Bring to the boil, then turn off the heat.

② Divide the fruit between four ramekins (custard cups) and chill.

③ Whisk the cream with the yoghurt and vanilla essence until thick.

④ When the fruit is cold, spread the cream mixture over the top of the fruit and chill for about an hour.

⑤ Thickly sprinkle the caster sugar over the top of the cream in each ramekin.

⑥ Place the ramekins under a preheated grill (broiler) so that the sugar caramelises, then chill them for about another hour so that the caramel layer is cold and crisp.

⑦ Serve cold with langue de chat biscuits.

PREPARATION TIME: 15 MINUTES PLUS CHILLING
COOKING TIME: 5 MINUTES

# PEACH MUESLI TORTE
## —— SERVES 8 ——

|  | METRIC | IMPERIAL | AMERICAN |
|---|---|---|---|
| Butter or margarine | 150 g | 5 oz | ⅔ cup |
| Caster (superfine) sugar | 25 g | 1 oz | 2 tbsp |
| Can of peach slices | 410 g | 14½ oz | 1 large |
| Light brown soft sugar | 100 g | 4 oz | 2 tbsp |
| Eggs, lightly beaten | 2 | 2 | 2 |
| Milk | 15 ml | 1 tbsp | 1 tbsp |
| Plain (all-purpose) flour | 75 g | 3 oz | ¾ cup |
| Muesli | 100 g | 4 oz | 1 cup |
| Baking powder | 7.5 ml | 1½ tsp | 1½ tsp |
| Ground cinnamon | 5 ml | 1 tsp | 1 tsp |
| Ground ginger | 2.5 ml | ½ tsp | ½ tsp |
| Greek yoghurt, to serve |  |  |  |

① Preheat the oven to 180°C/350°F/gas mark 4. Grease and line a 28 × 18 cm/11 × 7 in shallow cake tin (pan).

② Melt 25 g/1 oz/2 tbsp of the butter or margarine and stir in the caster sugar, then pour over the base of the cake tin. Arrange the sliced fruit on top.

③ Put the light brown soft sugar into a bowl with the remainder of the butter or margarine and beat together until creamy in consistency.

④ Gradually beat in the eggs and milk, then fold in the rest of the dry ingredients.

⑤ Carefully spoon the mixture over the fruit, level the surface, then place in the oven to bake for about 35 minutes or until the cake is firm to the touch.

⑥ Remove from the oven and allow to stand for 5 minutes before turning out on to a cooling rack. Serve warm with Greek yoghurt.

PREPARATION TIME: 15 MINUTES
COOKING TIME: 35 MINUTES

# APPLE MOULDS WITH FRESH RASPBERRY SAUCE

—— SERVES 6 ——

| | METRIC | IMPERIAL | AMERICAN |
|---|---|---|---|
| Cooking (tart) apples, peeled, cored and finely chopped | 450 g | 1 lb | 1 lb |
| Caster (superfine) sugar | 50 g | 2 oz | ¼ cup |
| Clear honey | 5 ml | 1 tsp | 1 tsp |
| Cinnamon stick | 1 | 1 | 1 |
| Ground cinnamon | 5 ml | 1 tsp | 1 tsp |
| Double (heavy) or whipping cream | 300 ml | ½ pt | 1¼ cups |
| Mascarpone cheese | 225 g | 8 oz | 1 cup |
| Vegetarian gelatine | 15 g | ½ oz | ½ oz |
| **For the sauce:** | | | |
| Fresh raspberries | 225 g | 8 oz | 8 oz |
| Icing (confectioners') sugar | 30 ml | 2 tbsp | 2 tbsp |
| Sprigs of fresh mint | 6 | 6 | 6 |
| Fresh raspberries, for decoration | 12 | 12 | 12 |

① Lightly oil the inside of six cups or ramekins (custard cups), then line each with a piece of clingfilm (plastic wrap) large enough to overlap the rims, ensuring that the inside is as smooth as possible.

② Place the apples in a saucepan with the sugar, honey and cinnamon stick. Cover with the saucepan lid and cook over a low heat until the apples are pulpy.

③ Remove the cinnamon stick and mash the apples with a fork. Mix in the ground cinnamon. Allow to cool.

④ Whisk the cream in a large bowl until it has thickened slightly.

⑤ Add the Mascarpone cheese to the cream and whisk together until quite thick.

⑥ Sprinkle the gelatine over about 30 ml/2 tbsp of very hot water in a cup. Leave for a few minutes, then stir briskly to ensure all the gelatine has dissolved. Allow to cool slightly.

⑦ Quickly whisk the cooled apple purée into the cream mixture, then whisk in the gelatine. Divide the mixture between the prepared cups chill to set. This will take at least 2 hours.

⑧ Meanwhile, prepare the sauce. Place the raspberries and icing sugar in a saucepan, cover and simmer gently for a few minutes until the fruit is just soft.

⑨ Liquidise the fruit, then pass through a sieve (strainer) to remove the pips. Cool.

⑩ Tip the apple moulds out on to individual serving plates and peel off the clingfilm and surround with a pool of sauce. Decorate each with a sprig of mint and a couple of raspberries.

PREPARATION TIME: 30 MINUTES PLUS SETTING
COOKING TIME: 10 MINUTES

# HONEYED CHOCOLATE DIP WITH FRESH FRUITS
—— SERVES 4 ——

|  | METRIC | IMPERIAL | AMERICAN |
|---|---|---|---|
| A selection of fresh fruit such as strawberries, nectarines, kiwi fruit, bananas, pineapple |  |  |  |
| Plain (semi-sweet) chocolate | 225 g | 8 oz | 8 oz |
| Double (heavy) or whipping cream | 90 ml | 6 tbsp | 6 tbsp |
| Clear honey | 30 ml | 2 tbsp | 2 tbsp |

① Wash and peel the fruit if necessary, and cut into bite-sized chunks or slices.

② Break the chocolate into pieces and put into a saucepan with the cream. Stir over a gentle heat until the chocolate melts.

③ Stir in the honey.

④ Serve the dip hot in a bowl, placed in the centre of a platter with the fresh fruit arranged around.

PREPARATION TIME: 15 MINUTES
COOKING TIME: 5 MINUTES

# STUFFED NECTARINE BRÛLÉE

#### —— SERVES 4 ——

|  | METRIC | IMPERIAL | AMERICAN |
|---|---|---|---|
| Large nectarines, peeled, stoned (pitted) and halved | 4 | 4 | 4 |
| Sweet white wine | 300 ml | ½ pt | 1¼ cups |
| Mascarpone cheese | 100 g | 4 oz | ½ cup |
| Ground almonds | 50 g | 2 oz | ⅓ cup |
| Icing (confectioners') sugar | 20 ml | 4 tsp | 4 tsp |
| Caster (superfine) sugar | 90 ml | 6 tbsp | 6 tbsp |

① Place the nectarine halves in a saucepan with the wine, cover and simmer for 10–15 minutes until the nectarines are just tender. Allow to cool slightly, then drain off the cooking liquid and reserve.

② Combine the cheese with the ground almonds and icing sugar.

③ Place spoonfuls of the mixture into the cavity of each nectarine and press down slightly to flatten.

④ Place the nectarines in a shallow flameproof dish. Sprinkle the surface of each nectarine thickly with the caster sugar. Place under a preheated grill (broiler) for several minutes to caramelise the sugar.

⑤ Serve straight away with a little of the wine cooking liquid spooned around.

PREPARATION TIME: 15 MINUTES
COOKING TIME: 15 MINUTES

# LUXURY MERINGUE NESTS
## —— SERVES 4 ——

| | METRIC | IMPERIAL | AMERICAN |
|---|---|---|---|
| Large bananas, sliced | 2 | 2 | 2 |
| Rum | 30 ml | 2 tbsp | 2 tbsp |
| Large meringue nests | 4 | 4 | 4 |
| Scoops of vanilla ice cream | 4 | 4 | 4 |
| *For the sauce:* | | | |
| Soft brown sugar | 30 ml | 2 tbsp | 2 tbsp |
| Butter or margarine | 30 ml | 2 tbsp | 2 tbsp |
| Golden (light corn) syrup | 15 ml | 1 tbsp | 1 tbsp |
| Double (heavy) cream | 75 ml | 5 tbsp | 5 tbsp |

①  Toss the bananas in the rum, then divide between the meringue nests.

②  Top each with a scoop of vanilla ice cream.

③  Heat the sugar, butter or margarine and syrup in a pan until melted.

④  Stir in the cream and quickly heat through.

⑤  Pour the hot sauce over the ice cream and serve.

PREPARATION TIME: 10 MINUTES
COOKING TIME: 5 MINUTES

# QUICK BAKES

Here is a selection of snacks and sweet treats which you can serve for afternoon tea, mid-morning coffee or packed lunches.

Some will also make perfect accompaniments for soups, starters and main courses. They have all been chosen for their wholesome ingredients so that they not only make tasty snacks but also add plenty of goodness into your vegetarian diet.

# CHOCOLATE OAT BISCUITS

## —— MAKES ABOUT 25 ——

|  | METRIC | IMPERIAL | AMERICAN |
|---|---|---|---|
| Rolled oats | 75 g | 3 oz | ¾ cup |
| Medium oatmeal | 50 g | 2 oz | ½ cup |
| Cocoa (unsweetened chocolate) powder | 15 ml | 1 tbsp | 1 tbsp |
| Soft brown sugar | 75 g | 3 oz | ⅓ cup |
| Oil | 120 ml | 4 fl oz | ½ cup |
| Egg, beaten | 1 | 1 | 1 |
| Plain (semi-sweet) chocolate, broken into small pieces | 100 g | 4 oz | 1 cup |

① Preheat the oven to 160°C/325°F/gas mark 3.

② Place the oats, oatmeal, cocoa, sugar and oil in a mixing bowl. Stir well and leave to stand for 15 minutes.

③ Add the egg and mix thoroughly.

④ Place teaspoonfuls of the mixture well apart on a greased baking (cookie) sheet and flatten with a palette knife.

⑤ Bake for 15–20 minutes until browned.

⑥ Leave to cool on the baking sheet for a couple of minutes, then transfer to a wire rack to cool completely.

⑦ Place the chocolate in a basin over a pan of very hot water and stir until melted.

⑧ Dip each biscuit (cookie) in the chocolate so that it is half coated, then leave on the cooling rack until the chocolate is set.

PREPARATION TIME: 10 MINUTES PLUS RESTING AND COOLING
COOKING TIME: 15–20 MINUTES

# DATE AND HONEY PANCAKES

—— MAKES ABOUT 20 ——

|  | METRIC | IMPERIAL | AMERICAN |
|---|---|---|---|
| Self-raising (self-rising) flour | 225 g | 8 oz | 2 cups |
| A pinch of salt |  |  |  |
| Egg | I | I | I |
| Clear honey | 30 ml | 2 tbsp | 2 tbsp |
| Milk | 300 ml | ½ pt | 1¼ cups |
| Dates, stoned (pitted) and chopped | 75 g | 3 oz | ½ cup |
| Butter or margarine, melted | 50 g | 2 oz | ½ cup |
| Extra butter and honey, to serve |  |  |  |

① Sift the flour and salt into a bowl and make a well in the middle.

② Break in the egg and add the honey and mix together.

③ Gradually beat in half the milk, working in the flour. Stir in the remaining milk and the dates.

④ Lightly brush a large, heavy frying pan (skillet) with some of the melted butter or margarine and heat.

⑤ Drop spoonfuls of the batter into the pan, about five at a time. Cook over a moderate heat until bubbles start to appear on the surface. Flip them over and cook for another few minutes.

⑥ Remove from the pan and keep warm. Use the batter to make more pancakes, greasing the pan, when necessary, with the melted butter or margarine.

⑦ Serve warm spread with extra butter and honey.

PREPARATION TIME: 5 MINUTES
COOKING TIME: 10 MINUTES

# PEAR AND SEMOLINA CAKE
## —— SERVES 6 ——

| | METRIC | IMPERIAL | AMERICAN |
|---|---|---|---|
| Self-raising (self-rising) flour | 175 g | 6 oz | 1½ cups |
| A pinch of salt | | | |
| Butter or block margarine | 100 g | 4 oz | ½ cup |
| Ground almonds | 25 g | 1 oz | ¼ cup |
| Semolina (cream of wheat) or polenta | 25 g | 1 oz | ¼ cup |
| Soft brown sugar | 100 g | 4 oz | ½ cup |
| Cinnamon | 2.5 ml | ½ tsp | ½ tsp |
| Pears, peeled, cored and cut into small pieces | 450 g | 1 lb | 1 lb |
| Eggs, lightly beaten | 2 | 2 | 2 |
| **For the topping:** | | | |
| Soft brown sugar | 25 g | 1 oz | ¼ cup |
| Ground cinnamon | 2.5 ml | ½ tsp | ½ tsp |
| Cream or butter, to serve | | | |

①　Preheat the oven to 200°C/400°F/gas mark 6.

②　Sift the flour and salt into a mixing bowl. Cut the fat into the flour and rub until the mixture resembles breadcrumbs.

③　Stir in the ground almonds, semolina or polenta, brown sugar and cinnamon. Stir the chopped pears into the flour mixture.

④　Mix in the beaten eggs.

⑤　Turn the mixture into a greased 20–23 cm/8–9 in cake tin (pan) and level off the top with the back of a spoon. Sprinkle with the brown sugar and cinnamon.

⑥　Bake in the oven for 30–40 minutes until a skewer inserted in the centre comes out clean. Allow the cake to shrink in the tin slightly before turning out on to a cooling rack.

⑦　Serve hot with cream, or split and serve buttered, hot or cold.

PREPARATION TIME: 15 MINUTES

COOKING TIME: 30–40 MINUTES

# WINDFALL APPLE AND WALNUT CAKE
## —— SERVES 6 ——

| | METRIC | IMPERIAL | AMERICAN |
|---|---|---|---|
| **For the topping:** | | | |
| Butter or margarine | 50 g | 2 oz | ¼ cup |
| Demerara sugar | 50 g | 2 oz | ¼ cup |
| Windfall apples, peeled, cored and sliced | 450 g | I lb | I lb |
| **For the cake:** | | | |
| Self-raising (self-rising) flour | 175 g | 6 oz | 1½ cups |
| Baking powder | 5 ml | I tsp | I tsp |
| Polenta | 50 g | 2 oz | ½ cup |
| Ground cinnamon | 5 ml | I tsp | I tsp |
| Butter or margarine | 50 g | 2 oz | ¼ cup |
| Soft brown sugar | 50 g | 2 oz | ¼ cup |
| Caster (superfine) sugar | 50 g | 2 oz | ¼ cup |
| Walnuts, roughly chopped | 50 g | 2 oz | ½ cup |
| Egg | I | I | I |
| Milk | 150 ml | ¼ pt | ⅔ cup |
| Whipped cream or Greek yoghurt, to serve | | | |

① Preheat the oven to 190°C/375°F/gas mark 5.

② For the topping, quickly melt the butter or margarine and sugar in the bottom of a 900 g/2 lb loaf tin (pan) over a high heat to caramelise the sugar. Add the apples and quickly toss in the mixture. Remove from the heat.

③ To make the cake, sift the flour and baking powder into a large bowl, then stir in the polenta and cinnamon. Rub in the butter or margarine until the mixture resembles fine breadcrumbs. Stir in the two kinds of sugar and the walnuts.

④ Add the beaten egg and milk and beat well with a wooden spoon to give a smooth batter. Pour over the apples.

⑤ Bake for 30–40 minutes until risen and the centre springs back when pressed, and turn out while still hot.

⑥ Serve hot with whipped cream or Greek yoghurt.

PREPARATION TIME: 15 MINUTES
COOKING TIME: 30–40 MINUTES

# HERBED OATCAKE SLICES

## —— MAKES 8 ——

| | METRIC | IMPERIAL | AMERICAN |
|---|---|---|---|
| Block margarine | 25 g | 1 oz | 2 tbsp |
| Boiling water | 90 ml | 6 tbsp | 6 tbsp |
| Medium oatmeal | 225 g | 8 oz | 2 cups |
| Dried rosemary | 1.5 ml | ¼ tsp | ¼ tsp |
| Dried oregano | 1.5 ml | ¼ tsp | ¼ tsp |
| Dried sage | 1.5 ml | ¼ tsp | ¼ tsp |
| Bicarbonate of soda (baking soda) | 1.5 ml | ¼ tsp | ¼ tsp |
| A pinch of salt | | | |
| Butter and a selection of cheeses, to serve | | | |

① Preheat the oven to 180°C/350°F/gas mark 4.

② Place the margarine and water in a small pan and heat until the margarine has melted. Cool.

③ Mix the oatmeal, herbs, bicarbonate of soda and salt together in a bowl. Stir in the cooled liquid and mix to a soft dough, adding a little more water, if necessary.

④ Pat the dough into a round about 20 cm/8 in in diameter. Place on an ungreased baking (cookie) tray.

⑤ Bake for about 40 minutes. Cut into eight wedges, then leave to cool slightly before turning on to a cooling rack. Serve buttered with a selection of cheeses.

PREPARATION TIME: 10 MINUTES
COOKING TIME: 40 MINUTES

# CHOCOLATE CHIP ROCK CAKES
## —— MAKES ABOUT 20 ——

|  | METRIC | IMPERIAL | AMERICAN |
|---|---|---|---|
| Self-raising (self-rising) flour | 225 g | 8 oz | 2 cups |
| Block margarine | 150 g | 5 oz | ⅔ cup |
| Caster (superfine) sugar | 150 g | 5 oz | ⅔ cup |
| Chocolate chips | 100 g | 4 oz | 1 cup |
| Egg | 1 | 1 | 1 |
| A little milk |  |  |  |
| Oil, for greasing |  |  |  |

① Preheat the oven to 220°C/425°F/gas mark 7.

② Sift the flour, then rub in the margarine until the mixture resembles breadcrumbs. Stir in the sugar and chocolate chips. Stir in the egg and enough milk to give a fairly stiff consistency.

③ Place heaped spoonfuls well apart on greased baking (cookie) trays.

④ Bake for about 10 minutes until firm and golden brown.

PREPARATION TIME: 10 MINUTES
COOKING TIME: 10 MINUTES

# CHOCOLATE MUESLI FRIDGE CAKE
## —— MAKES 8 SLICES ——

|  | METRIC | IMPERIAL | AMERICAN |
|---|---|---|---|
| Plain (semi-sweet) chocolate, broken into pieces | 150 g | 5 oz | 1¼ cups |
| Butter or margarine | 15 ml | 1 tbsp | 1 tbsp |
| Golden (light corn) syrup | 15 ml | 1 tbsp | 1 tbsp |
| Soft brown sugar | 15 ml | 1 tbsp | 1 tbsp |
| Muesli | 50 g | 2 oz | ½ cup |

① Place all the ingredients, apart from the muesli, in a saucepan and heat gently until the chocolate has melted.

② Stir in the muesli.

③ Pour the mixture into a loose-bottomed 18 cm/7 in cake tin (pan). Smooth the surface. Chill for several hours until firm.

④ Cut into slices and serve with afternoon tea or as a dessert with cream.

PREPARATION TIME: 5 MINUTES PLUS CHILLING

# CHEESE AND CHIVE BITES

—— MAKES 25–30 ——

|  | METRIC | IMPERIAL | AMERICAN |
|---|---|---|---|
| Cheddar cheese, finely grated | 100 g | 4 oz | 1 cup |
| Mustard powder | 2.5 ml | ½ tsp | ½ tsp |
| Plain (all-purpose) flour | 15 ml | 1 tbsp | 1 tbsp |
| A pinch of celery salt |  |  |  |
| Freshly ground black pepper |  |  |  |
| Snipped fresh chives | 5 ml | 1 tsp | 1 tsp |
| Milk | 5 ml | 1 tsp | 1 tsp |

① Preheat the oven to 200°C/400°F/gas mark 6.

② Combine the cheese, dry ingredients and chives. Stir in the milk.

③ Using your hands, squeeze the mixture into balls about the size of a marble and place well apart on a baking (cookie) tray. Flatten the balls slightly with the back of a spoon.

④ Bake for about 5–6 minutes or until well browned.

⑤ Remove from the baking tray while still warm and place on a cooling rack. Serve as nibbles or to accompany soup.

PREPARATION TIME: 5 MINUTES
COOKING TIME: 5–6 MINUTES

# PIZZA WHEEL BAKES

—— MAKES ABOUT 20 ——

|  | METRIC | IMPERIAL | AMERICAN |
|---|---|---|---|
| Packet of pizza dough mix | 140 g | 5 oz | 1 |
| Tomato purée (paste) | 45 ml | 3 tbsp | 3 tbsp |
| Onion, finely chopped | 1 | 1 | 1 |
| Small red (bell) pepper, finely diced | ½ | ½ | ½ |
| Dried oregano | 5 ml | 1 tsp | 1 tsp |
| Strong Cheddar cheese, grated | 175 g | 6 oz | 1½ cups |

① Preheat the oven to 220°C/425°F/gas mark 7.

② Make up the pizza dough according to the packet instructions, then roll out to a rectangle about 20 × 28 cm/8 × 11 in.

③ Spread the tomato purée over the dough, then sprinkle over the other ingredients, finishing with the cheese. Roll up from the long edge to form a sausage. Cut into about 20 slices.

④ Place each slice cut side down on a baking (cookie) sheet and flatten slightly with a palette knife.

⑤ Bake for about 10 minutes or until the dough is firm and browned. Serve as a teatime treat or as part of a party buffet.

PREPARATION TIME: 10 MINUTES
COOKING TIME: 10 MINUTES

# SPICED CHAPATTIS

—— MAKES 8 ——

|  | METRIC | IMPERIAL | AMERICAN |
|---|---|---|---|
| Plain (all-purpose) wholemeal flour | 450 g | I lb | 4 cups |
| Chilli powder | 5 ml | I tsp | I tsp |
| Ground cumin | 2.5 ml | ½ tsp | ½ tsp |
| Ground turmeric | 2.5 ml | ½ tsp | ½ tsp |
| Salt and freshly ground black pepper |  |  |  |
| Garlic purée (paste) | 5 ml | I tsp | I tsp |
| Tomato purée | 5 ml | I tsp | I tsp |
| A little warm water |  |  |  |

①  Place the flour in a bowl with the dried spices and seasoning. Gradually work in the garlic and tomato purées with a little warm water, using your hands. Add more warm water and work in until the mixture forms a smooth dough.

②  Knead on a floured work surface for at least 5 minutes until it is pliable and smooth. Leave to rest for about 10 minutes.

③  Knead again briefly, then form the dough into a sausage and cut into eight equal-sized pieces. Roll each piece into a ball, then, on a floured board, roll out to a thin pancake about 15 cm/6 in across.

④  Heat a heavy-based frying pan (skillet) until very hot. Place one chapatti in the pan and cook for a minute or two. Flip over and cook the other side. Repeat this process with the other chapattis.

⑤  Serve warm with curries, casseroles or even a crisp mixed salad.

PREPARATION TIME: 25 MINUTES

COOKING TIME: 5 MINUTES

# CHEESE AND HERB SODA BUNS
## —— MAKES 8 ——

|  | METRIC | IMPERIAL | AMERICAN |
|---|---|---|---|
| Wholemeal flour | 225 g | 8 oz | 2 cups |
| Plain (all-purpose) flour | 225 g | 8 oz | 2 cups |
| Salt | 10 ml | 2 tsp | 2 tsp |
| Bicarbonate of soda (baking soda) | 10 ml | 2 tsp | 2 tsp |
| Butter or margarine | 50 g | 2 oz | ¼ cup |
| Dried basil | 5 ml | 1 tsp | 1 tsp |
| Dried oregano | 5 ml | 1 tsp | 1 tsp |
| Dried parsley | 5 ml | 1 tsp | 1 tsp |
| Milk, plus extra for glazing | 300 ml | ½ pt | 1¼ cups |
| Lemon juice | 15 ml | 1 tbsp | 1 tbsp |
| Strong Cheddar cheese, grated | 50 g | 2 oz | ½ cup |
| Butter or margarine, to serve |  |  |  |

① Preheat the oven to 200°C/400°F/gas mark 6.

② Sift the flours, salt and bicarbonate of soda into a mixing bowl. Cut in the fat and rub in until the mixture resembles breadcrumbs. Stir in the herbs.

③ Combine the milk and lemon juice and add sufficient to the dry mix to form a soft dough. Knead on a floured surface until smooth and elastic.

④ Divide into eight equal pieces and roll into balls.

⑤ Place on a floured baking (cookie) tray, leaving room in between for the rolls to spread. Brush with milk and sprinkle with the grated cheese.

⑥ Bake for about 20 minutes until risen and golden brown.

⑦ Serve hot or cold spread with butter or margarine.

PREPARATION TIME: 10 MINUTES
COOKING TIME: 20 MINUTES

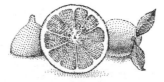

# INDEX

almonds
  middle eastern dream dessert 106
  pear and semolina cake 117
  tagliatelle with toasted nut sauce 57
apple
  apple moulds with fresh raspberry sauce 110–11
  butterscotch apple pancakes 100–1
  leek and pepper loaf with apple 54–5
  potato, swede and apple straw cakes 65
  quick plum and apple fool 99
  walnut-dressed coleslaw 92
  windfall apple and walnut cake 118
artichokes
  in balsamic vinegar and orange 68
  with savoury butter 81
asparagus pâté 10
aubergine (eggplant)
  garlic and aubergine tomatoes 75
  Mediterranean picnic loaf 39
  pimiento and aubergine rolls 13
avocado
  avocado and mushroom flan 59
  borlotti bean salsa salad 90
  olive and avocado vol-au-vents 23
  spiced bean and avocado rafts 29
  with sun-dried tomatoes 16

baked beans
  beany drop scones 76
  potato brunch tarts 60–1
banana
  coffee and tia maria bombe 97
  luxury meringue nests 113
beans
  bean and rice moulds 72
  spiced bean and avocado rafts 29
  see also types of beans e.g. baked beans
beansprouts
  Chinese vegetables in peanut mayonnaise 89
  and nut salad 86
beany drop scones 76
beetroot
  baby beetroot in a cheese sauce 27
  tomato Parmesan salad with root crisps 93
biscuits
  chocolate chestnut castles 107
  layered rhubarb crips with gingered cream 103
blackberry, mixed berry brûlée 108
blueberry, mixed berry brûlée 108
borlotti beans
  mushroom borlotti stroganoff 42
  salsa salad 90
bread
  cheese and chutney doughnuts 62

Mediterranean picnic loaf 39
  spiced bean and avocado rafts 29
brie, spaghetti with 52
broad (fava) beans
  country carrots 66
broccoli and cauliflower korma 33
brussel sprouts
  brussel sprout and chestnut soufflé 50
  squeaky cakes 79
butter (lima) bean and tomato salad 91
butterscotch apple pancakes 100–1

cabbage
  juniper cream 72–3
  Savoy mushroom parcels 38
  squeaky cakes 79
  walnut-dressed coleslaw 92
Camembert salad, crunchy 87
Carol's green salad 84
carrot
  country carrots 66
  garden vegetables with parsley stock 71
  and herb sausages 32
  roast roots with fresh herbs 63
  and spinach moulds 78
  Szechuan carrots 70
  tomato Parmesan salad with root crisps 93
  vegetable casserole with tomato cobbler 52
  walnut-dressed coleslaw 92
  winter casserole with mustard dumplings 26–7
casserole
  vegetable casserole with tomato cobbler 52
  winter casserole with mustard dumplings 26–7
cauliflower
  broccoli and cauliflower korma 33
  and walnut soup 19
celery
  and mushrooms with boursin 73
  and sweetcorn pancakes 30–3
  winter casserole with mustard dumplings 26–7
chapattis, spiced 123
cheddar cheese
  carrot and herb sausages 32
  cheese and chive bites 121
  cheese and chutney doughnuts 62
  cheese and herb soda buns 124
  cider soup with paprika 22
  pizza wheel bakes 122
cheese
  gnocchi alla romana 40
  and lentil cutlets 47
  see also types of cheese e.g. Camembert
cherries with cinnamon, mulled 105
chestnut

brussel sprout and chestnut soufflé 50–1
chocolate chestnut castles 107
and parsnip turnovers 48
chick peas (garbanzos)
quick felafels 34
spicy chick pea dip with crudites 12
chilli
borlotti bean salsa salad 90
sunshine rice 43
Thai-style mixed vegetables 37
Chinese vegetables in peanut mayonnaise 89
chocolate
chocolate chestnut castles 107
chocolate chip rock cakes 120
chocolate muesli fridge cake 120–1
chocolate oat biscuits 115
honeyed chocolate dip with fresh fruits 111
chutney
cheese and chutney doughnuts 62
cider soup with paprika 22
citrus onion marmalade 74
coconut
broccoli and cauliflower korma 33
pineapple in caramelised coconut sauce 101
Thai-style mixed vegetables 37
coffee and tia maria bombe 97
corn fritters with sun-dried tomato sauce 49
country carrots 66
courgette (zucchini)
Carol's green salad 84
cheesy courgettes with redcurrant sauce 20
Mediterranean picnic loaf 39
watercress and courgette soup with stilton 14
cream cheese
asparagus pâté 10
see also garlic and herb cream cheese
crunchy curried parsnips 77
cucumber
cucumber raita 28
with dill soured cream 94

date and honey pancakes 116

egg noodles
mango and noodle salad 83
summer vegetable chow mein 58
eggplant see aubergine
eggs
brussel sprout and chestnut soufflé 50–1
mustard potato frittata 46
potato brunch tarts 60–1

fava beans see broad beans
felafels, quick 34
filberts see hazelnuts
flageolet red salad 94–5
French (green) beans
Carol's green salad 84
summer vegetable chow mein 58
in a zesty lime sauce 80

fresh herb potato salad 85

garbanzos see chick peas
garden vegetables with parsley stock 71
garlic and herb cream cheese
avocado and mushroom flan 59
celery and mushrooms with boursin 73
pimiento and aubergine rolls 13
ginger
melon with stem ginger 10
warm gingered tofu salad 88
gnocchi alla romana 40
gooseberry oatmeal medley 98
green beans see French (green) beans

hazelnuts (filberts)
beansprout and nut salad 86
gooseberry oatmeal medley 98
herbed oatcake slices 119
honey
date and honey pancakes 116
honey peach yoghurt ice 104
honeyed chocolate dip with fresh fruits 111
horseradish mayonnaise 95
hummus and garlic mushroom pie 56–7

ice cream
luxury meringue nests 113

juniper cream cabbage 72–3

leek
gingered leek filo tarts 18
leek and pepper loaf with apple 54–5
Thai-style mixed vegetables 37
lemon
lemon Parmesan peas 68
lentils
cheese and lentil cutlets 47
Persian squash with peppers 25
quick felafels 34
red lentils in a soured cream dressing 86–7
sunshine rice 43
vegetable casserole with tomato cobbler 52
lettuce, Carol's green salad 84
lima bean see butter (lima) bean
lime sauce, French beans in a zesty 80
luxury meringue nests 113

mangetout (snow peas)
Chinese vegetables in peanut mayonnaise 89
summer vegetable chow mein 58
Thai-style mixed vegetables 37
warm gingered tofu salad 88
mango and noodle salad 83
marrow see squash
Mascarpone cheese
apple moulds with fresh raspberry sauce 110–11
Mascarpone pears with brandy pistachios 21
stuffed nectarine brûlée 112

mayonnaise
  horseradish 95
  peanut 89
Mediterranean picnic loaf 39
melon with stem ginger 10
meringue
  coffee and Tia Maria bombe 97
  luxury meringue nests 113
middle eastern dream dessert 106
minted pea soup in a moment 11
mixed berry brûlée 108
Mozzarella cheese
  baby beetroots in a cheese sauce 27
  Mediterranean picnic loaf 39
muesli torte, peach 109
mulled cherries with cinnamon 105
mushrooms 73
  avocado and mushroom flan 59
  creamy garlic mushroom pitta pockets 35
  curried filo purses 15
  hummus and garlic mushroom pie 56–7
  mixed mushrooms in a red wine sauce 31
  mushroom borlotti stroganoff 42
  potato brunch tarts 60–61
  Savoy mushroom parcels 38
  vegetable casserole with tomato cobbler 52
  winter casserole with mustard dumplings 26–7

nectarine
  beansprout and nut salad 86
  stuffed nectarine brûlée 112
nuts
  beansprout and nut salad 86
  tagliatelle with toasted nut sauce 57
  see also types of nut e.g. walnut

oatmeal
  gooseberry oatmeal medley 98
  herbed oatcake slices 119
oat biscuits, chocolate 115
olives
  olive and avocado vol-au-vents 23
  rustic potatoes 69
onion marmalade, citrus 74
orange
  artichokes in balsamic vinegar and orange 68
  citrus onion marmalade 74

Parmesan cheese
  baby beetroots in a cheese sauce 27
  cheesy courgettes with redcurrant sauce 20
  Italian spinach salad 91
  lemon Parmesan peas 68
  three-pepper lasagne 44–5
  tomato Parmesan salad with root crisps 93
parsnip
  chestnut and parsnip turnovers 48
  crunchy curried parsnips 77
  honeyed parsnips with mustard sauce 67
  roast roots with fresh herbs 63

tomato Parmesan salad with root crisps 93
  vegetable casserole with tomato cobbler 52
  winter casserole with mustard dumplings 26–7
pasta
  crunchy Camembert salad 87
  fusilli with spinach 55
  spaghetti with brie 52
  tagliatelle with toasted nut sauce 57
pastries
  avocado and mushroom flan 59
  chestnut and parsnip turnovers 48
  curried filo purses 15
  gingered leek filo tarts 18
  hummus and garlic mushroom pie 56–7
  potato brunch tarts 60–61
peach
  honey peach yoghurt ice 104
  peach muesli torte 109
peanuts
  beansprout and nut salad 86
  peanut mayonnaise 89
pear
  Mascarpone pears with brandy pistachios 21
  pear and semolina cake 117
peas
  garden vegetables with parsley stock 71
  lemon Parmesan 68
  minted pea soup in a moment 11
  see also types of peas e.g. chick peas
pepper
  borlotti bean salsa salad 90
  Carol's green salad 84
  Chinese vegetables in peanut mayonnaise 89
  flageolet red salad 94–5
  gnocchi alla romana 40
  leek and pepper loaf with apple 54–5
  Mediterranean picnic loaf 39
  Persian squash with peppers 25
  pizza wheel bakes 122
  potato brunch tarts 60–1
  roast roots with fresh herbs 63
  sunshine rice 43
  three-pepper lasagne 44–45
pesto potato cakes 66–7
pimiento and aubergine rolls 13
pine kernels
  fusilli with spinach 55
  Italian spinach salad 91
pineapple in caramelised coconut sauce 101
pistachio nuts
  Mascarpone pears with brandy pistachios 21
  pitta pockets, creamy garlic mushroom 35
pizza wheel bakes 122
plum and apple fool, quick 99
potato
  fresh herb potato salad 85
  mustard potato frittata 46
  pesto potato cakes 66–7
  potato, swede and apple straw cakes 65
  potato brunch tarts 60–1

potato salad with horseradish mayonnaise 95
rustic potatoes 69
squeaky cakes 79
pulses, vegetable casserole with tomato cobbler 52

quark, honey peach yoghurt ice 104

radishes, Chinese vegetables in peanut mayonnaise 89
raspberry
    apple moulds with fresh raspberry sauce 110–11
    mixed berry brûlée 108
    swiss raspberry layers 102
redcurrant sauce, cheesy courgettes with 20
rhubarb crisp with gingered cream, layered 103
rice
    bean and rice moulds 72
    middle eastern dream dessert 106
    mild curried risotto with cucumber raita 28
    sunshine rice 43
roast roots with fresh herbs 63
rutabaga, see swede

salsa salad, borlotti bean 90
sausages, carrot and herb 32
semolina (cream of wheat)
    gnocchi alla romana 40
    pear and semolina cake 117
shallots
    ball marrow with shallot topping 36
    garden vegetables with parsley stock 71
    Savoy mushroom parcels 38
snow peas, see mangetout
soups
    cauliflower and walnut soups 19
    cider soup with paprika 22
    minted pea soup in a moment 11
    tomato and basil soup with oregano 17
    watercress and courgette soup with stilton 14
soured (dairy sour) cream
    cucumber with dill 94
    red lentils in a soured cream dressing 86–7
    spicy chick pea dip with crudités 12
spicy chick pea dip with crudités 12
spinach
    carrot and spinach moulds 78
    fusilli with spinach 55
    Italian spinach salad 91
    summer vegetable chow mein 58
spring onions (scallions)
    Carol's green salad 84
    Chinese vegetables in peanut mayonnaise 89
    Italian spinach salad 91
    potato salad with horseradish mayonnaise 95
    quick felafels 34
    Thai-style mixed vegetables 37
squash (marrow)
    Persian squash with peppers 25
    with shallot topping 36
squeaky cakes 79
stilton cheese

watercress and courgette soup with
    stilton 14
strawberry, mixed berry brûlée 108
stuffed nectarine brûlée 112
summer vegetable chow mein 58
swede (rutabaga)
    potato, swede and apple straw cakes 65
    winter casserole with mustard dumplings 26–7
sweetcorn
    celery and sweeetcorn pancakes 30–1
    Chinese vegetables in peanut mayonnaise 89
    corn fritters with sun-dried tomato sauce 49
    mango and noodle salad 83
    summer vegetable chow mein
    Thai-style mixed vegetables 37
    warm gingered tofu salad 88
Swiss raspberry layers 102
Szechuan carrots 70

Thai-style mixed vegetables 37
Tia Maria bombe, coffee and 97
tofu salad, warm gingered 88
tomatoes
    avocado with sun-dried tomatoes 16
    bean and rice moulds 72
    butter bean and tomato salad 91
    corn fritters with sun-dried tomato sauce 49
    garlic and aubergine tomatoes 75
    gnocchi alla romana 40
    sunshine rice 43
    three-pepper lasagne 44–45
    tomato and basil pizza 61
    tomato and basil soup with oregano 17
    tomato Parmesan salad with root crisps 93
    vegetable casserole with tomato cobbler 52
    winter casserole with mustard dumplings 26–7
turnips
    garden vegetables with parsley stock 71
    roast roots with fresh herbs 63

vegetable casserole with tomato cobbler 52

walnut
    beansprout and nut salad 86
    cauliflower and walnut soup
    crunchy Camembert salad 87
    tagliatelle with toasted nut sauce 57
    walnut-dressed coleslaw 92
    windfall apple and walnut cake 118
watercress and courgette soup with stilton 14
winter casserole with mustard dumplings 26–7

yoghurt
    gooseberry oatmeal medley 98
    honey peach yoghurt ice 104
    mixed berry brûlée 108
    quick plum and apple fool 99

zucchini see courgette